CLEARING THE HURDLES

Issues and Answers in Middle School Sports

C. Kenneth McEwin   John Swaim

National Middle School Association
Westerville, Ohio

Betty Edwards, Executive Director
Jeff Ward, Deputy Executive Director
April Tibbles, Director of Publications
Edward Brazee, Editor, Professional Publications
John Lounsbury, Consulting Editor, Professional Publications
Mary Mitchell, Designer, Editorial Assistant
Dawn Williams, Publications Manager
Lindsay Kronmiller, Graphic Designer
Nikia Reveal, Graphic Designer
Marcia Meade-Hurst, Senior Publications Representative
Peggy Rajala, Publications Marketing/Ad Sales Coordinator

Library of Congress Cataloging-in-Publication Data
McEwin, C. Kenneth
   Clearing the hurdles: issues and answers in middle school sports/C. Kenneth McEwin and John Swaim
       p. cm.
   Includes bibliographical references.
   ISBN 978-156090-213-3
  1. School sports--United States. 2. Physical education and training--United States. 3. Middle school education--United States. I. Swaim, John. II. Title.
GV346.M43 2007
796.071--dc22   2007033259

National Middle School Association
4151 Executive Parkway, Suite 300
Westerville, Ohio 43081
1-800-528-NMSA f: 614-895-4750
www.nmsa.org

NMSA®

Contents

About the Authors

Yesterday...

The athletic careers of Ken McEwin and John Swaim were nothing like the sports experiences of young adolescents today. Yet they each remark that their middle level sports experiences were significant in their lives.

Growing up in small-town Chicota, Texas, Ken's first formal sports experience was not until ninth grade when he made the varsity basketball team; he then had a successful high school basketball and track career. Before high school, sports for Ken were informal, playing "scrubs" at school, an invented game of softball that included every student, with rules to fit the situation. Until ninth grade, softball and volleyball games were always co-ed and occurred during recess. There were no organized sports programs available in the community.

John also played basketball, although track was his passion. With his father, a Hall of Fame track coach, he attended track meets before he began competing himself in his Kansas City junior high school. John was always interested in sports, but prior to grade seven, everything was sandlot ball—after school, weekends, and summers. Fifty years later, he remembers the disappointment of being selected as an alternate for his seventh grade basketball team. However, by ninth grade he had become a starter. John later became a successful college track athlete at Emporia State in Kansas and then a swimming and track coach.

Today...

Dr. C. Kenneth McEwin is professor and coordinator of middle grades teacher education at Appalachian State University, Boone, North Carolina. He is a former sixth grade teacher and school principal, with extensive experience consulting with schools, districts, state departments, higher education institutions, and policymaking bodies. A former National Middle School Association president, he has received a number of awards including the John H. Lounsbury Distinguished Service Award.

Dr. John Swaim recently retired from Otterbein College, Westerville, Ohio, as a professor of education. He is also professor emeritus at the University of Northern Colorado, where he served 25 years in the UNC Laboratory School as the founding middle school principal and as an area head in the College of Education. John has been instrumental in securing middle level certification in several states and is widely known for his work in middle level education. He served as president of National Middle School Association and received the John H. Lounsbury Distinguished Service Award.

FOREWORD

Let's Put the Fun Back in Middle School Sports

Ah, the good old days of sports ... when kids learned to play basketball, or baseball, or tennis on their own, shooting baskets on the playground or in their driveway ... when kids didn't specialize in one sport while still preteens ... when parents were seen but seldom heard at the games ... when kids actually played sports without adults' organizing leagues, conducting tryouts, buying uniforms, choosing most valuable players, and awarding trophies. The reality is that in most places, those days are long gone. And that is exactly why *Clearing the Hurdles—Issues and Answers in Middle School Sports* is such an important resource for schools, parents, and anyone interested in middle level sports.

As middle school interscholastic sports expanded while intramurals floundered, physical education teachers and coaches were left largely to their own devices. Middle schools now have a responsibility to thoughtfully assess these programs and find the rightful place for sports in developmentally responsive, total school programs. The old questions are still relevant and need answers: Are middle level sports only for talented and gifted athletes—or everyone? Are sports extracurricular, cocurricular, or simply part of the everyday curriculum? Should middle schools provide appropriate sports experiences for all young adolescents that will help them grow, in sports, as schools do in every other curriculum area? What preparation and philosophy should middle school coaches possess? How should parents be involved, and how can they be supportive?

This book by well-known middle level education leaders Ken McEwin and John Swaim answers these critical questions. The authors provide a comprehensive look at middle school sports and make the case that sports programs must be treated as any other program in middle schools—fully supported, open to all, and most importantly, based on the best principles of what is appropriate for young adolescents.

Fortunately for us, the authors have done their homework, conducting a national survey to determine the status of middle school sports programs and drawing on the literature to provide current information on all aspects of this topic. Chapter 3 brings us up-to-date information on sports injuries, psychological considerations, the increasing amount of attrition in sports, the use of middle school programs as farm clubs for high schools, and much more. This chapter and the one to follow alone are well worth the cost of this resource. Chapter 4 deals with developmentally responsive middle level sports programs and provides many specific ideas about modifying rules, providing participation-based sports, limiting the season and post-season, offering club and community sports programs to augment school programs, and revamping eligibility issues.

For too long, middle school sports have been left alone to provide highly valued entertainment in small towns and suburbs, serve as feeder programs for high schools, and satisfy parents' desires for their girls' and boys' athletic success. Middle school sports experiences are, indeed, important—but in different ways and for different purposes from high school or college sports. While all other aspects of middle schools have come under close scrutiny for their worth and ability to promote academic achievement and be in line with the nature of young adolescents, sports programs for the most part have continued to operate with little direction.

Every middle level school needs to reexamine and assess its sports programs, and this book provides the information needed to carry out such a project. We must clear the hurdles to make sports in every middle school a happy experience, where all youngsters will participate in a variety of sports, develop their skills, and revel in the camaraderie and sense of team that comes with participating in sports.

—Edward N. Brazee
August 2007

1.
MIDDLE LEVEL SPORTS
AND THE MIDDLE SCHOOL CONCEPT

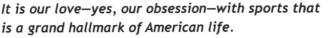

*It is our love—yes, our obsession—with sports that
is a grand hallmark of American life.*

—*Sports Done Right*

O rganized sports have become a dominant feature of our culture. From tee ball for tots to professional teams performing in mega-stadiums, sports touches almost every American's life—and pocketbook. Almost all educational institutions above the elementary level support athletic teams in one or more sports that are followed intently, not only by the students and their parents but by the community. Middle schools, which came on the scene beginning in the 1960s, are no exception. The nation embraced the concept of establishing schools that were specifically designed for young adolescents. These middle schools represent efforts to create and maintain learning environments that capitalize on the nature and needs of young adolescents.

There are now more than 14,000 public middle level schools in the U.S. The increase in the number of grades six through eight middle schools and the corresponding decrease in the number of grades seven through nine junior high schools have been especially dramatic in the last 25 years. Additionally, there are more than 3,000 pre-K/K-8 public elementary schools that house young adolescents enrolled in grades five through eight.

Middle level schools have implemented at varying levels the curriculum, programs, and practices championed by middle school authorities that are backed by research and successful practice (McEwin, Dickinson, & Jenkins, 2003). A clearly articulated set of programs, practices, curricular priorities, and other components essential to highly successful middle schools has been articulated in the literature and is frequently called the middle school concept or the middle school philosophy (Anfara, Andrews, & Mertens, 2005; Erb, 2005; George & Alexander, 2003; National Middle School Association, 2003).

The overall goal of all middle level programs is to meet the varied needs of every young adolescent by being developmentally responsive, academically challenging, and socially equitable (National Forum to Accelerate Middle Grades Reform, n.d.). This vision includes but is certainly not limited to the preparation of young adolescents for senior high school. Far from it, for middle schools have been unapologetically committed to serving the broad goals of a full education. Many of today's middle schools have created their own identity and become highly successful by focusing on the students they serve. Unfortunately, however, in most middle schools, the interscholastic sports programs have not followed the lead of these developmentally responsive middle schools; and they do not reflect the way these interscholastic programs are organized. Too many middle schools have created and maintained competitive sports programs that mimic high school and college level competitive sports.

Perceptions of Middle School Interscholastic Sports

Just what is the proper role of sports in middle level schools? This sometimes perplexing question has been asked and discussed by middle school advocates, sports enthusiasts, and others for decades. It is an even more burning question for those who are both middle school advocates and middle school sports enthusiasts. In many cases, however, the question has not even been raised because of the prevailing assumption that traditional sports programs and practices serve young adolescents well. In other cases, educators who know that interscholastic sports programs should be developmentally responsive back away from advocating needed changes because they fear being unpopular with those who strongly support such programs—community members, parents of successful athletes, coaches, the press. Others believe that the middle school philosophy is appropriate for the classroom, but should not be a consideration in competitive athletic programs. But there are a few others who believe that middle school sports should be developmentally responsive and fully reflect the middle school philosophy, period!

Parent perceptions

The way parents answer the question of the proper place of sports in the middle school seems to hinge on their prior experience with sports. For example, middle school parents who were themselves good athletes tend to hold the traditional view that sports should prepare their children for successful participation in high school athletics, and they believe middle school sports should be a feeder system for senior high school sports. Usually the children of these parents have themselves already been involved in organized sports for several years and see middle school sports as a stepping stone to the next level of sports specialization.

There are other parents who value their children's participation in sports, but place less emphasis on its competitive aspect. These parents view middle school interscholastic sports primarily as something their children will enjoy and learn from and provide them with opportunities to see if they have an interest in or a special talent for a particular sport.

Middle school educator perceptions

Not only do parents have varying perceptions about the nature of middle school sports, but so do middle school teachers, coaches, and administrators. It should not be assumed that educators in these positions automatically support developmentally responsive interscholastic sports programs. The faculty and administration of many middle schools hold a common vision for their school built around the needs and characteristics of young adolescents. However, when it comes to sports, that same vision often does not apply. Large numbers of teachers, administrators, coaches, and athletic directors are acknowledged advocates of the middle school philosophy in the classroom but not on the athletic field. There are, however, growing numbers of middle school teachers, coaches, administrators, and other stakeholders who are now striving to make their intramural and interscholastic sports programs more developmentally responsive.

Student athlete perceptions

Middle school student athletes are in the process of building their own attitudes about sports. They understand the high stakes associated with trying out for interscholastic sports and may believe that, if they are cut, they have no future in sports. Tryouts frequently lead to some young adolescents' experiencing a feeling of inadequacy that causes them to give up on any future participation in sports. There is often a sense that if they are not one of the best, there is little use in trying out in the future. Carrying this type of reasoning one step further, some young adolescents and their parents believe they must specialize in one sport to be successful enough to play at the high school level and beyond. Unfortunately, these decisions are often made before the student athletes have a chance to find out in which sport they might have the most talent. Many times these decisions are made for them by their parents before they even enter middle school.

Being on a team and interacting with peers is a valuable learning experience. Student athletes not only want to find out what potential they might have in a sport, they want also to interact with their peers in a common experience, one that makes them part of a special group.

Because the major focus of the world of young adolescents is in the here and now, they need opportunities to be successful in the present instead of always being asked to think about future possibilities. Asking them to work positively based on future possibilities can be inappropriate and result in undue stress. Future sports opportunities will come their way soon enough without taking away the enjoyment of the sports moment they are currently experiencing. This does not mean that young adolescents should not have aspirations for the future when participating in competitive sports, but rather that the major emphasis should be having healthy and enjoyable sports experiences with their peers.

Because the major focus of the world of young adolescents is in the here and now, they need opportunities to be successful in the present instead of always being asked to think about future possibilities.

The points just presented apply just as much to gifted young adolescent athletes as to their less-talented peers. Too often, gifted athletes get an inflated and unrealistic view of themselves based on interactions with peers and adults who treat them differently because of their early athletic abilities. The most common reason for athletic success at a young age is early physical maturation. As their peers get older and become more physically mature, some student athletes begin to lose their competitive edge and are no longer the standouts they once were. It is important that talented student athletes be given opportunities to realize their full abilities while in middle school, but it is also important that they enjoy participating without undue concern over what might be expected of them in the future. Setting goals is a part of participation in competitive sports, but goals should be well grounded in the present.

The Middle School Philosophy and Middle School Sports

It is commonly said that perception is reality. What people believe to be true is, indeed, reality to them. The same might be said about schools. The perceptions of those working in schools regarding the way these schools should be organized and operated are based on their beliefs and the experiences life has brought them (e.g., educational experiences in schools and cultural backgrounds). Their resulting beliefs—their philosophies and dispositions—are powerful factors in their daily interactions with students, fellow educators, and others. The diverse beliefs faculty members and other educators have initially can be merged into a clearly articulated vision and school philosophy that go beyond rhetoric to carefully planned and articulated implementation.

This We Believe (NMSA, 2003) notes that a shared vision guides decisions at highly successful middle schools. It is important to have the total middle level program, including intramural and interscholastic sports, reflect the shared middle school vision and philosophy. Differing perceptions about middle school sports that sometimes exist within and outside the middle schools should not exempt these programs from reflecting the vision and philosophy of schools designed to serve young adolescents.

> *It is important to have the total middle level program, including intramural and interscholastic sports, reflect the shared middle school vision and philosophy.*

Levels of implementation

For purposes of presentation, the authors have classified the relationship of middle school sports programs to the overall philosophy of the school in three ways:

- Middle schools that subscribe to the middle school philosophy and have developmentally responsive sports programs that reflect that philosophy.
- Middle schools that subscribe to the middle school philosophy but have sports programs that are not developmentally responsive and do not reflect that philosophy.
- Middle schools that neither subscribe to a middle school philosophy nor have sports programs that are developmentally responsive.

Looking at middle school sports from these three perspectives, two of the models are clearly not in the best interest of young adolescents. Part of the reason for this reality is that establishing and maintaining effective middle school sports programs is usually controversial and never easy. Since virtually all middle schools have interscholastic sports programs (96%), decisions go beyond simply choosing between an intramural and an interscholastic sports program. As will be discussed more fully in later chapters, the authors support middle schools having both intramural and interscholastic sports programs, both driven by a developmentally responsive philosophy. Although the issues surrounding middle school sports are complex, the fundamental question is actually very simple. Can all middle school sports programs be made developmentally responsive for young adolescents?

Middle schools and middle level programs in other grade organizations have continued to struggle to escape the shadows of junior high schools and senior high schools and to establish and maintain an identity as schools devoted to serving young adolescents. One of the major tenets of the middle school concept has been to fit the school

Track is offered for both boys and girls in 71 percent of middle schools that have interscholastic programs.

to young adolescents, not young adolescents to the school. Despite the difficulty of changing traditions and old assumptions, significant progress has been made in moving away from the glorified elementary school and miniature senior high models of schooling. Educators at most middle schools are providing school environments that reflect the intellectual, physical, social, and emotional characteristics of young adolescents. However, as noted earlier, this same transformation has not occurred as consistently with regard to middle school sports as sports programs that conflict with the developmental characteristics of young adolescents continue to exist. Unfortunately for young adolescents, modifying traditional, highly competitive interscholastic sports programs has been deemed virtually unapproachable in many middle schools. The adults responsible for these programs have been unwilling to consider or take the steps necessary to make interscholastic sports better reflect what is known about the developmental stage of early adolescence.

This situation calls for a full examination of the question: What are the implications of the middle school concept for middle school sports programs? The following section briefly describes the implications using *This We Believe* (NMSA, 2003) as a framework. Each of these implications is addressed in more detail in the remaining chapters.

Implications of Middle School Components on Middle School Sports

This *We Believe* Statements	Implications for Middle School Sports
Successful schools for young adolescents are characterized by a culture that includes	
Educators who value working with this age group and are prepared to do so.	Coaches and others involved in middle school sports should be thoroughly knowledgeable about not only the physical development of young adolescents, but also their social, emotional, and intellectual development. They should be aware of the implications of these characteristics for coaching and make decisions based on this knowledge. Professional development opportunities should be sought out that provide current knowledge about the developmental characteristics of young adolescents and ways to use this knowledge to help them benefit from participation in sports.
Courageous, collaborative leadership.	Changes needed to make middle school sports more appropriate for young adolescents require collaborative and courageous leadership on the part of administrators, coaches, and others responsible for middle school sports programs. Unfortunately, middle school sports programs not designed to be responsive to the developmental needs of young adolescents become entrenched within the school and community.
A shared vision that guides decisions.	Various individuals and groups have vested interests in middle school sports that conflict with this vision, including student athletes, coaches, parents, administrators, and athletic directors. For a middle school sports program to be successful, all stakeholders must understand and support the purposes of sports programs and make decisions based on that understanding. Open and continual dialogue contributes to the development of a philosophy that helps make intramural and interscholastic sports programs developmentally responsive through the establishment of widely understood and successfully implemented visions and philosophies.
An inviting, supportive, and safe environment.	Middle school sports programs should be available to all young adolescents who wish to participate. The focus should be on the fundamentals of the sport and the enjoyment of participation. Since young adolescents are especially susceptible to physical injuries, every attempt should be made to make sports participation as safe as possible.
High expectations for every member of the learning community.	Too frequently, high expectations in middle school sports have been defined by a team or individual's win-loss record. This often leads to a win-at-all-costs approach and the exclusion of less-talented athletes from participation. High expectations in middle school sports should mean helping each young adolescent who chooses to participate to work toward reaching his or her potential in the sport selected.
Students engaged in active learning.	Young adolescents who participate in sports should have opportunities to be actively engaged. Practices and games should be organized in ways that provide all athletes maximum opportunities to participate. Activities should be planned to allow all participants to learn and practice the skills required.

This We Believe Statements	Implications for Middle School Sports
An adult advocate for every student.	The contacts coaches have with young adolescents provide ideal opportunities to get to know them well and serve as adult advocates. Coaches are in a position to advocate for student athletes on the playing field and also in other aspects of their lives. The top priority of all middle school coaches should be the welfare of the young adolescents rather than the win-loss records of individuals or teams.
School-initiated family and community partnerships.	Middle school sports provide parents with opportunities to observe their children's participation at school. It is important that schools inform parents about the purposes of school-sponsored sports programs and the conditions under which they operate; it is also important that schools provide ways for parents to be positively involved in sports programs. Although this participation may be limited primarily to observation, there are other ways for them to provide support (e.g., appropriate behavior at games, realistic expectations for success, positive support for their children). Gaining the support of parents for developmentally responsive sports programs is a prerequisite for achieving middle school intramural and interscholastic sports programs that serve all young adolescents well.
Successful schools for young adolescents provide	

Curriculum that is relevant, challenging, integrative, and exploratory.	Sports are designed to create challenges for those who participate. The challenge of breaking records is a major part of sports, but attempts to break records is too often emphasized instead of the importance of successful participation of individual young adolescents. The challenges faced in sports by middle school age youth should focus more on improvements gained than on comparisons with accomplishments of past athletes.
	    At the middle school level, young adolescents should be provided with multiple opportunities to explore their interests and abilities for several sports rather than being pushed to select one while ignoring others. Exploring several sports allows young adolescents to discover and further develop skills to participate successfully in middle school sports for which they have talent and potential for future success.
	    High quality middle school sports programs provide opportunities that extend beyond traditional team sports to life sports (e.g., skiing, golf, tennis, walking). These sports programs also offer opportunities for physical activities to be included in curricular units (e.g., Olympics, fitness).

Multiple learning and teaching approaches that respond to their diversity.	Coaches should use multiple teaching strategies to help young adolescents learn to be successful in sports while taking into account their diverse interests and abilities. Although sports provide opportunities to be actively involved, active involvement alone is sometimes not sufficient. Young adolescents can lose interest if practices are boring no matter how much physical activity is involved. Many opportunities for assessment, including self-assessment, should be provided.

This We Believe Statements	Implications for Middle School Sports
Assessment and evaluation programs that promote quality learning.	One criticism of middle school sports is that there is too much pressure placed on athletes to win—not only from coaches, but also from parents and community members. As coaches assess and evaluate the talents and skills of young adolescents participating in sports programs, it is crucial that they remember the overall goals of middle school sports. Coaches should continually remind young athletes of their progress while helping them face the challenges that accompany sports participation.
Organizational structures that support meaningful relationships and learning.	The way middle schools sports programs are organized and administered is profoundly important to establishing and maintaining developmentally responsive programs and practices. Middle school sports programs should operate with rules and regulations that best serve this developmental age group rather than using ones designed for the high school level. Intramural sports programs should be adequately funded and organized and play a prominent role in the overall middle school sports program.
School-wide efforts and policies that foster health, wellness, and safety.	Sports programs should be carefully organized to provide playing environments that are safe and reflect the priorities of sports participation that contribute to the health and wellness of all young adolescents. Conditioning is an important part of sports. However, too frequently, exercises and drills become the focus of practices rather than skill development and enjoyment. Middle school sports should maintain a balance between activities designed for conditioning and learning skills that allow athletes to be successful. Of course, athletes should have sufficient conditioning to allow them to participate in sports without the fear of being injured.
Multifaceted guidance and support services.	Coaches have opportunities to provide guidance and support for middle school athletes both on and off the playing field, although they should not bear primary responsibility for providing guidance and support. Coaches may not have the specialized expertise or time to provide guidance individually for all individuals under their supervision. They can, however, help identify young adolescents who need guidance and help them get the assistance they need. The trust that develops between coaches and their players in developmentally responsive sports programs encourages relationships that increase the likelihood that middle school students will ask them for help and advice. Sports participation may also open doors for closer relationships between teachers and students in both interscholastic and intramural settings.

In Summary

This book explores the issues surrounding sports at the middle level. It advances ways that middle school sports programs can become more responsive to the developmental characteristics, needs, and interests of young adolescents. Middle schools sports should be integral parts of the school's vision and purpose—not parallel or separate.

Depending on the perceptions readers already have about the role of middle school sports, this book will likely either affirm or challenge those perceptions. For those who believe middle school sports should be built on the developmental characteristics of young adolescents, this book will be affirming; but for those who believe that middle school sports should emphasize competition and be a feeder system for the high school, this book may prove to be challenging. Whatever the perceptions of readers, the authors hope to bring attention to the current situation and to focus attention on what needs to be done to improve middle school sports. It is hoped that the book will narrow rather than widen the divide that exists between those on either side of the issue.

The authors had four specific purposes for writing this book. First, the authors wanted to determine the status of middle school sports in public middle level schools across the nation. To obtain this information, a national study was conducted—apparently the first national survey ever conducted that focused exclusively on middle school sports programs and practices. Chapter 2 reports the results of this study, which provides a knowledge base about current practices and foundational data for the recommendations made in the concluding chapter.

A second reason for writing this book was to provide a comprehensive literature review of what is known about sports programs for young adolescents. Readers should find this wealth of updated information useful in increasing their own knowledge about key issues related to sports programs at the middle school level and informing related decisions. The knowledge gained from the literature review helped shape the recommendations found in Chapter 7.

A third purpose was to provide readers with some examples of successful intramural and interscholastic sports programs. Readers will find succinct descriptions of successful programs found in several chapters. The schools are identified so that readers may contact them for additional information if desired. Study of these successful programs also influenced the recommendations made.

A final and major purpose of the book was to specifically address the major issues surrounding middle school sports and provide recommendations that would guide the needed reexamination of middle school sports. These issues were identified in the national survey, from a review of the current and historical literature and from the authors' experiences.

Although these four purposes drove the creation of this book, there are numerous other related issues that arose and are discussed. The authors hope readers will find this book informative and that it will provide guidance in efforts to organize and implement middle level intramural and interscholastic sports programs that are developmentally responsive. ●

2.
THE STATUS OF MIDDLE LEVEL SPORTS

When Did Sports Become So Complicated?

As a seventh-grader in 1960, I played football, basketball, and baseball at my junior high school in southeastern Michigan. Sports were fun. The best part for me was having a uniform and being part of a team. While my memories may be hazy about parent involvement, I do remember that when some parents attended the games, they spent most of their time talking to each other in the stands. No parent ever questioned a coach about lack of playing time or position played. We moved from season to season with most kids playing all sports. I never attended a summer sports camp; that was time for playing sandlot ball—without adults, uniforms, or championships. We formed our own teams, created new games when we didn't have enough people to play the regular game, and learned to settle our own disputes as they inevitably arose. No one ever talked about specializing in one sport to receive a college scholarship. Sports were sports—fun and recreational, and they kept us physically active and out of trouble.

— A 59-year-old teacher educator

Since the 1960s, there have been rather dramatic changes in nearly every aspect of our lives. This includes the way sports are conducted, not only in our middle and high schools, but in our community recreational programs. To be able to understand, assess, and evaluate middle school sports programs, it is necessary to determine exactly what is the status of middle level sports programs and practices in the nation's middle schools. To answer this basic question, the authors conducted a national survey. Data from this study, presented here, will give readers the information they need to interpret and react to views expressed in subsequent chapters.

A National Study of Middle School Sports
Programs and Practices

Surveys requesting information about middle school sports programs were mailed to 1,239 randomly selected middle schools during the 2002-2003 school year. This number represented 10 percent of all public middle schools in the U.S. that housed grades 5-8, 6-8, or 7-8. Schools with these grade configurations were selected because most young adolescents attend middle level schools with one of these grade organizational plans. Three hundred forty-six middle schools (30%) returned completed surveys.

Forty-one percent of responding schools were located in rural settings, 21 percent in urban areas, and 38 percent in suburban communities. Nine percent of responses were received from grades 5-8 middle schools, 75 percent from grades 6-8 middle schools, and 16 percent from middle level schools housing grades 7-8.

The size of student populations of responding schools closely approximated patterns found in a previous national survey of middle schools (McEwin, Dickinson, & Jenkins, 2003). As shown in Table 1, the most common student enrollment size was between 601 and 800. Sixty-one percent of all schools enrolled between 201 and 800 students (24%). There were large schools represented in the random sample, with 18 percent enrolling 1,001 or more students. The total number of students in the smallest responding school was 74; the largest had 2,092 students. The mean size of all schools was 687.

Table 1
Number and Percent of Enrollments of Middle Schools

Enrollment	Number	Percent
1-200	22	6
201-400	62	18
401-600	65	19
601-800	84	24
801-1,000	52	15
1,001-1,200	34	10
1,201-1,400	18	5
More than 1,400	9	3
Totals	346	100

Intramural sports

Although participating in intramural sports programs opens the benefits of physical activity and involvement in sports to large numbers of young adolescents, only 58 percent of middle level schools in the study had intramural sports programs. As shown in Table 2, in schools with intramural programs, the most popular sport offered for both boys and girls was basketball (98%). Volleyball was the next most frequently provided intramural sport for girls (64%) and boys (57%). Forty-five percent of schools offered soccer for boys and 43 percent for girls. Touch football was also a relatively frequently available sport for boys (40%), as was softball for girls (38%).

Table 2
Percent of Middle Schools with Intramural Sports
Offering Selected Sports for Boys and Girls

Sports	Boys	Girls
Baseball	12	<1
Basketball	98	98
Cross Country	14	14
Football (Tackle)	5	2
Football (Touch)	40	29
Gymnastics	7	7
Soccer	45	43
Softball	26	38
Swimming	1	1
Tennis	19	22
Track	21	21
Volleyball	57	64
Wrestling	17	5
Other	31	31

Thirty-one percent of schools indicated that sports other than the choices provided in the survey were part of the intramural sports programs at their schools. The most frequently reported sports added were floor hockey (45%), field hockey (26%), table tennis (24%), golf (17%), and lacrosse (14%). About one in ten schools with intramural sports programs also listed archery, cheerleading, bowling, kickball, street hockey, or weight training.

Interscholastic sports

The percentage of middle schools with interscholastic (interschool) sports programs has increased dramatically since the beginning of the middle school movement (Figure 1). The percentage of public middle schools with interscholastic sports programs has increased from 50 percent in 1968, to 77 percent in 1993, to 96 percent in 2002 (Alexander, 1968; McEwin, Dickinson, & Jenkins, 1996, 2003). Results from the present study revealed that 96 percent of all middle schools have interscholastic sports programs, which is an identical percentage to that found in a national study in 2001 (McEwin, Dickinson, & Jenkins, 2003).

Figure 1
Percent of Middle Schools with Interscholastic Sports

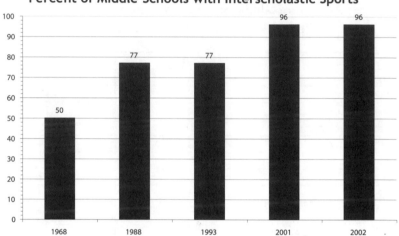

Respondents were asked to indicate which sports were included in their interscholastic sports programs. Table 3 presents a summary of responses received. The percentages shown are representative of all responding schools, not just the 96 percent that had interscholastic sports programs.

The most popular interscholastic sports for both boys and girls was basketball (92%). Basketball was also found to be the most frequently offered interscholastic sport in a 2001 national study of middle schools (McEwin, Dickinson, & Jenkins, 2003) as well as in a national survey of middle grades programs and practices in grades K-8 schools (McEwin, Dickinson, & Jacobson, 2004). Seventy-one percent of middle schools also offered track, the second most frequently offered sport for boys and girls. Almost identical percentages of schools reported offering cross-country for boys (48%) and girls (47%). About four in ten schools also reported offering soccer for boys and girls. After these sports, the most often provided interscholastic sports were different for boys and girls (Table 3, Figures 2 and 3). For example, 62 percent of schools offered interscholastic tackle football for boys and 9 percent for girls. Forty-five percent of schools offered wrestling for boys and 15 percent for girls.

Table 3
Percent of Middle Schools with Selected Interscholastic Sports for Boys and Girls

Sports	Boys	Girls
Baseball	36	2
Basketball	92	92
Cross Country	48	47
Football (Tackle)	62	9
Football (Touch)	4	<1
Gymnastics	1	4
Soccer	40	39
Softball	5	42
Swimming	11	11
Tennis	20	20
Track	71	71
Volleyball	18	65
Wrestling	45	15
Other	16	28

Figure 2
Percent of Middle Schools with Selected Interscholastic Sports for Boys

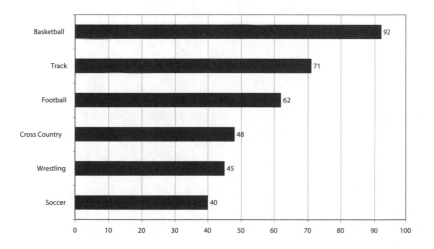

Figure 3
Percent of Middle Schools with Selected Interscholastic Sports for Girls

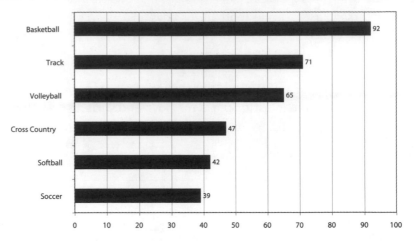

Interscholastic sports more traditionally considered appropriate for females were more frequently offered at middle schools rather than were those more commonly considered "male sports" (Table 3). For example, 65 percent of schools offered volleyball for girls with only 18 percent doing so for boys. Softball was provided for girls at 42 percent of middle schools with only 5 percent offering the sport for boys. Likewise, only 2 percent of schools provided baseball for girls as compared to 36 percent for boys. However, as shown in Table 3, some middle schools allow females to participate in sports that have been traditionally considered by many to be "male sports" (e.g., football, 9%).

Respondents were asked to indicate if interscholastic sports not included as options in the survey were provided and to list those sports. Sixteen percent indicated "yes" for boys and 28 percent "yes" for girls. The percentages of schools that listed additional interscholastic sports were 48 percent for cheerleading, 34 percent for field hockey, 27 percent for golf, 15 percent for lacrosse, and 10 percent for table tennis.

Scheduling intramural and interscholastic sports

Respondents were asked when intramural and interscholastic sports were scheduled at their schools. Sixty-four percent of respondents reported that intramurals were scheduled after regular school hours, 28 percent during school hours, and 8 percent at other times (e.g., weekends) (Figure 4). Ninety-six percent of middle schools scheduled interscholastic competition after school as compared to only 4 percent during school hours.

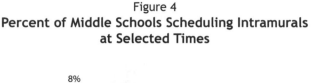

Figure 4
Percent of Middle Schools Scheduling Intramurals
at Selected Times

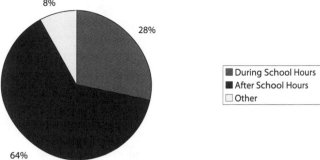

8%

28%

64%

- During School Hours
- After School Hours
- Other

The roles of intramural and interscholastic sports

Respondents were asked their opinions regarding whether middle schools should provide only intramural sports or only interscholastic sports, or if both types of sports programs should be available at this level. Eighty-three percent of respondents believed that middle schools should have both intramural and interscholastic sports programs. Eleven percent expressed a belief that only interscholastic sports should be provided, while six percent believed that only intramurals should be provided at the middle school level.

Respondents were also asked to indicate their opinions concerning which grades, if any, should be allowed to participate in interscholastic sports programs. As shown in Table 4, a small percentage of respondents thought that interscholastic sports should be available at the fifth grade level (7%), and two percent indicated that interscholastic sports should not be available at any middle grade level (grades 5-8). About one-third favored interscholastic sports for sixth grade, with more than nine of ten supporting interscholastic sports for older young adolescents enrolled in grades seven and eight.

No-cut interscholastic sports and rules modification policies

Ten percent of schools participating in the study had no-cut policies for all interscholastic sports. The most frequently offered no-cut sports were track (14%), football (12%), and cross-country (9%) (see Figure 5).

Table 4
**Number and Percent of Respondents Believing Interscholastic
Sports Should Be Offered at Specific Grade Levels**

	Number	Percent
Should Not Be Offered	6	2
Fifth Grade Level	24	7
Sixth Grade Level	128	36
Seventh Grade Level	329	92
Eighth Grade Level	359	94

Figure 5
**Percent of Middle Schools Listing Examples
of No-Cut Interscholastic Sports**

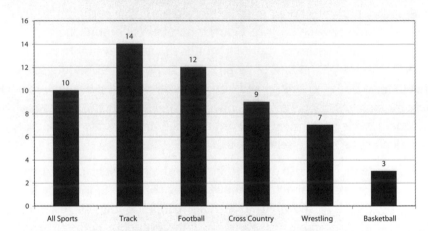

Respondents from the majority (57%) of middle schools with interscholastic sports programs reported that sports rules are sometimes modified to make them more compatible with the developmental stage of early adolescence. Examples of these modifications are listed below:

- Shorten track
- Shorten game lengths
- Limit schedule of games for all sports
- Establish an "everyone must play each game" policy
- Reduce size of playing field
- Limit number of events an individual can enter
- Schedule games played on schools days early
- Establish five quarters with rotating squads

- Provide A, B, and C teams in some sports
- Play second quarter rule in basketball
- Have A and B teams in football, volleyball, and basketball
- Use the "mercy" rule in football and basketball when one team is far ahead

Examples of modified sports play rules provided by respondents that are specific to selected sports:

Basketball
- Shorter playing time
- No press rule
- Smaller basketballs
- Score cleared each quarter

Baseball
- Pitching distance
- Size of baseball field adjusted
- Fewer innings
- Limit number of innings pitched

Football
- No metal spikes
- Everybody plays
- No blitzes
- No kick-offs
- Coaches on field with seventh grade team

Track
- Shorter distances
- Length of cross-country course
- No hurdles in track
- No pole vault in track
- Smaller shot
- Different spacing of hurdles or lower hurdles

Volleyball
- Five hits per side
- Serve close to net when necessary

Wrestling
- Weight classes modified
- Coaches allowed to be at edge of mat near athletes

Caribou Middle School

Phone: 207.493.4240

http://www.caribouschools.org/Middle/middle.html

Caribou Middle School—
A Developmentally Responsive Sports Program

Caribou Middle School (ME) is a grades five through eight school with an enrollment of 450 students. The school, which is in a rural farming community near the Canadian border, was constructed in the 1920s and presents various challenges to academic, cocurricular, and sports programming. These challenges are overcome by offering students innovative programming and creative scheduling that result in excellent educational opportunities. Caribou Middle School educators are committed to the premise of developmental assets as defined by Search Institute to create an atmosphere of support and high expectations for all young adolescents. They believe that developmentally appropriate activities increase student success in all aspects of their middle school experience. This belief extends to all aspects of the school, including academic, cocurricular, and sports programs.

Caribou Middle School's athletic program provides a variety of sports experiences for all students. The ability of Caribou Middle School to balance developmentally responsive activities with an appropriate level of competitiveness is widely respected in Maine. Caribou collaborates with the Recreation Department, Caribou High School teams, and the Maine Winter Sports Center to create high quality experiences for student athletes. These partnerships provide the necessary support and additional expertise needed to enhance the athletic experience of all students.

Caribou athletic philosophy

The overall philosophy of the athletic programs at CMS is to build character, citizenship, and teamwork. Coaches work daily to connect with student athletes on an individual basis and get to know who they are as individuals. Educators at Caribou understand the sensitivity associated with the developmental milestones middle school athletes experience and are diligent in making sure young adolescents walk away from athletic programs with positive experiences. For example, rosters for cut sports are never posted after tryouts. Additionally, coaches are required to counsel students individually when they do not make a sports team. They explain to individuals why they did not make the team, suggest skill areas they might work on to improve their performances, and point out practice opportunities that are available to help them improve their skills.

The sports program

The competitive sports program is divided into four seasons. The first season runs from August to October and includes seventh and eighth grade boys and girls soccer teams. It also includes no-cut boys and girls cross-country teams. The second season, November through February, includes boys and girls basketball, with separate teams for seventh and eighth graders, and cheerleading, with two squads comprised of both boys and girls in seventh and eighth grade. The late winter sports season is February and March and includes Nordic skiing and wrestling. Both of these no-cut sports are open to all students in grades five through eight. The Nordic program works with the Maine Winter Sports Center to outfit athletes with equipment at a low cost. Although this season is short, more than 100 students typically participate. The final sports season lasts from mid-April until late May. Sports offered include boys and girls track for fifth graders, tennis for seventh and eighth grade girls and boys, girls softball for seventh and eighth grade, and boys baseball for seventh and eighth grade students. The track program is a no-cut sport, with about 50 students typically participating.

Here are some additional highlights of the Caribou Middle School sports program:

- When students decide to participate on an athletic team, they are required to read a booklet about Caribou's athletic policies with their parents that highlights policies students are required to follow.
- Students must be passing all subjects to participate in sports. The athletic director completes bi-weekly grade checks on each athlete during each sports season. If a student is failing, teachers inform the athletic director, who informs the athlete and the athlete's parents. The student cannot continue participating until he or she is passing all classes. If a student-athlete is unable to maintain passing grades (70 and higher) for more than two grade checks, that athlete is no longer allowed to participate. This policy has proven to be very successful. Many times, a student athlete's highest academic average is maintained during a sports season.
- A plaque is awarded to the team that maintains the highest academic average. Many coaches believe that this award is the most important award a team can receive. Educators at Caribou pride themselves on the high academic averages that sports teams maintain. It is not uncommon for the lowest academic team average to be an 85—a tribute to CMS athletes and their coaches, teachers, and parents.
- Student athletes develop a sense of pride and positive self-concepts and are respected by their peers and teachers. They are required to dress up on game days. This is a way for them to stand out and be recognized for their hard work.
- Athletic awards are given to each student based on the number of years of participation. First-year athletes receive a certificate and a letter; second-year athletes receive a certificate and a trophy. Third-year students receive a certificate and a plaque. Four-year athletes receive a certificate and a sports-specific medallion. Student-athletes receive all awards at an evening awards night following their respective sports season. All students who have participated receive an award.
- The coaching staff at CMS is comprised mostly of teachers. This benefits the sports program and the athletes who participate in it. The hope to build scholar athletes is even more solidified when coaches are teachers. These coaches go above and beyond their duties by commonly offering what is known as "study hours" at CMS. These study hours are held in the teacher-coaches' classrooms at the conclusion of the school day and before practices begin after school. All coaches stress to athletes that academics are the priority, and frequently coaches become a struggling student's strongest resource for assistance and encouragement.
- Coaches receive training in first aid and cardiopulmonary resuscitation as well as automated external defibrillators. Most coaches are certified and have received training in coaching principles. An athletic trainer from the local hospital is employed to provide injury diagnosis, prevention, and treatment for all sports.

● ● ●

Participation in school, community, and club sports programs

Eighty-two percent of respondents noted that community or club sports programs offered some of the same sports sponsored by their schools. Only 14 percent of these schools reported that they have cooperative agreements with community or club sports programs. Sixty-nine percent of middle schools in the study allow young adolescents to participate in both school and community-based sports programs. An additional 15 percent allow students to participate in both types of programs as long as the sports played are not the same. Responses also showed that 11 percent of the schools do not allow participation in both kinds of competitive sports programs (Table 5).

Respondents from 63 percent of schools believed that the availability of community and club sports had no effect on the level of participation in interscholastic sports. Respondents from 21 percent of schools believed that these programs decreased participation in school-sponsored interscholastic programs, whereas 16 percent thought community or club programs increased participation in interscholastics.

Table 5

Percent of Middle Schools with Selected Policies Regarding Participation in School and Community or Club Sports Programs

Participation Policy	Percent
Students Can Participate in School and Community Sports Programs	69
Students Can Participate in School and Community Sports Programs if Not the Same Sport	15
Students Cannot Participate in Both School and Community Sports Programs	11
Other	5
Total	100

Student recognition programs

Ninety-two percent of schools with interscholastic sports programs had some form of formal student recognition for athletic success. The most common methods were the presentation of varsity letters (95%), certificates of participation (86%), and outstanding performance awards (44%). One-fourth of schools also presented team spirit awards. Additional examples provided by respondents included sports banquets, parties, announcements at school, trophies, sports assemblies, pin ceremonies, and sports jackets. The majority of school representatives also reported that the results of sports competitions were published in local newspapers (51%).

Middle school coaching

In the majority of schools (51%), between 91 and 100 percent of coaches were licensed (certified) teachers. In an additional 25 percent of middle schools, between 71 and 90 percent of coaches had teaching licenses. Percentages at the remaining 24 percent of schools, however, were low, with 4 percent of schools having only 0 to 10 percent of coaches who were licensed teachers (Table 6).

Table 6
Percent of Middle Schools Reporting Coaches
Who Are Licensed Teachers

Number	Percent
0-10	4
11-20	2
21-30	3
31-40	2
41-50	8
51-60	2
61-70	3
71-80	11
81-90	14
91-100	51
Totals	101

Approximately six in ten coaches had received formal first aid training, and 14 percent of schools had 71 to 90 percent of coaches with first aid training. However, the remaining 26 percent of schools had low percentages of coaches with the training. For example, seven percent of schools had between 0 and 20 percent of coaches with first aid training (Table 7). Information regarding compensation for coaches was also collected from respondents. Although coaches in 4 percent of schools received no additional compensation for coaching, 84 percent of schools reported that between 91 and 100 percent of their coaches were compensated (Table 8).

Middle school sports philosophy

Eighty-six percent of school respondents reported that they had a philosophy guiding their interscholastic sports programs, but only 25 percent reported that it was a formal, written sports philosophy. The most common methods of informing stakeholders about this philosophy was holding meetings with athletes and their parents at the beginning of each sport season and including the philosophy in policy handbooks (52%). Forty-seven percent of respondents indicated that their sports philosophy was included in the school handbook, with an additional 37 percent discussing it in meetings with athletes and their parents at the beginning of the school year. Of the 25 percent of schools with formal middle school sports philosophies, only 27 percent of respondents stated that the sports philosophy at their school was compatible with that of the majority of other schools with whom they competed.

Table 7
**Percent of Middle Schools with Coaches Who
Have First Aid Training**

Number	Percent
0-10	5
11-20	2
21-30	3
31-40	1
41-50	10
51-60	3
61-70	1
71-80	9
81-90	5
91-100	60
Totals	99

Table 8
**Percent of Middle Schools Reporting
Coaches Compensated Through
Additional Contracts**

Number	Percent
0-10	4
11-20	<1
21-30	<1
31-40	<1
41-50	1
51-60	<1
61-70	1
71-80	4
81-90	4
91-100	84
Totals	98

Respondents' views regarding middle school sports programs

Respondents were asked to express their views regarding middle school sports in a series of eight statements (Table 9). Choices provided were strongly agree, agree, disagree, and strongly disagree. The majority of respondents agreed or strongly agreed that obtaining funding for interscholastic sports (51%) and intramural sports (58%) is difficult (Figure 6a). When asked about the levels of community support for interscholastic and intramural sports, 83 percent of respondents agreed or strongly agreed that interscholastic sports were strongly supported by the community as compared to only 46 percent indicating strong community support for intramural sports programs (Figure 6a). As shown in Table 9, only 7 percent of respondents strongly agreed that community support for intramural sports programs was strong as compared to 45 percent for interscholastic sports.

Table 9
Percent of Respondents' Views Regarding Selected Aspects of Middle School Sports Programs

	Strongly Agree	Agree	Disagree	Strongly Disagree
Obtaining funding for interschool sports is difficult	16	35	36	13
Obtaining funding for intramural sports is difficult	24	34	30	12
Interschool sports are strongly supported by the community	45	38	9	8
Intramural sports are strongly supported by The community	7	39	41	13
Finding coaches knowledgeable about young adolescent development is difficult	16	45	31	8
Sports facilities for interschool sports are adequate	16	40	26	18
Coaches and others are aware of high injury rates among young adolescents	11	63	25	1
Parents and community members are aware of high injury rates among young adolescents	7	55	33	5

Sixty-one percent agreed or strongly agreed that finding coaches knowledgeable about young adolescent development is difficult (Figure 6b). The majority (56%) agreed or strongly agreed that sports facilities for middle school interscholastic sports are adequate (Table 9 and Figure 6b). Almost three-fourths (74%) agreed or strongly agreed that coaches are aware of the high rate of injuries among young adolescents participating in middle school interscholastic sports programs (Figure 6b). Sixty-two percent also agreed or strongly agreed with the statement that parents and community members are aware of the high injury rates among middle school athletics (Table 9 and Figure 6b).

Figure 6a
Percent of Respondents Agreeing with Selected Statements

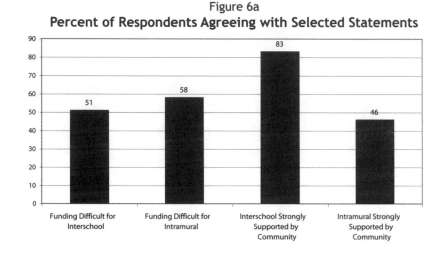

Figure 6b
Percent of Respondents Agreeing with Selected Statements

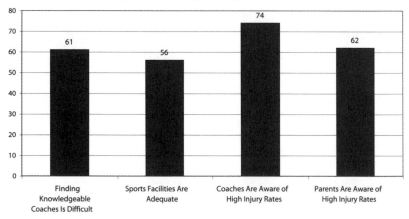

William Thomas Middle School—Creative Solutions

William Thomas Middle School, located in the small farming community of American Falls, Idaho, has an enrollment of 375, seventy percent of whom are economically disadvantaged. The student body is 55 percent Caucasian, 40 percent Hispanic, and 5 percent Native American. Prior to 1995, WTMS had a traditional sports program where about half of those who wanted to play were cut. In 1995 a committee of staff, parents, and community members met to make a plan that would allow more students to participate in both school and community-sponsored programs. The resulting plan, which allowed for wider participation while maintaining interscholastic sports, required changes not only at WTMS, but also at five schools in other districts in the sports league.

The plan involves having up to 24 middle level students on a team. On game days, athletes are divided into two or three teams of equal ability. The seventh grade plays at one school while the eighth grade plays at the other. This plan works well because all players are on the same teams, have the same coaches, and practice together. This means that young adolescents do not feel they have been placed on teams with less prestige, but rather that they play in different games. Having teams where abilities are more closely matched has resulted in many closely contested games that are exciting to participants, fans, cheerleaders, and others.

- A six-year study was conducted to evaluate the effects of the new sports plan on senior high school varsity sports. The past sports history of starting varsity players was examined. Results showed that in basketball 32 percent of high school starters played in the lower ability level games in seventh grade. In volleyball 37 percent of high school starters played in the lower ability level games. Data from this study indicate that in addition to the importance of including as many students as possible, wider participation in middle school sports actually provides significant benefits to high school sports programs.
- WTMS works closely with the community recreation department to ensure wide participation. Sign-up dates are announced, sports facilities are used without charge, and assistance is provided in finding qualified coaches. In addition to the obvious benefits of working closely with the community recreation department, it is important that positive relationships are ongoing in case the school district drops middle school interscholastic sports programs and community-sponsored sports are the only ones available.
- All students who complete cheerleader try-out requirements make the squad. Requirements include making a poster, attending two weeks of early morning training, performing an individual cheer, working with a group to create a group cheer, and performing a group cheer. All cheerleaders perform together in parades and at school assemblies, but are assigned to squads for different sports. This allows girls to participate in sports and be cheerleaders. Educators at WTMS have found that middle school students need to participate in different activities to see what they may really be interested in rather than becoming specialized in one area.
- Participation levels for girls volleyball is 32 percent, boys and girls basketball 34 percent, track 32 percent, and cheerleading 28 percent. Percentages of involvement are also high in community-sponsored football (41%), baseball (16%), and sixth grade basketball (38%).

William Thomas Middle School

Phone: 208.226.5206

http://www.wtms. sd381.k12.id.us/

Values placed on selected factors when employing coaches

   Respondents were also asked to respond to a series of statements focusing on the levels of importance placed on selected aspects of criteria when employing interscholastic coaches. Possible responses included essential, very important, important, and not important. One-hundred percent of respondents agreed that knowledge of the sport, the ability to motivate athletes, organizational skills, and the ability to communicate with parents were important, very important, or essential (Table 10 and Figure 7). Almost all respondents also believed that having a competitive spirit, having first aid training, and having knowledge of young adolescent development were essential, very important, or important (Figure 7). As shown in Table 10, the statements that most often received the rating of essential were competitive spirit, knowledge of young adolescent development, ability to motivate athletes, and first aid training.

Table 10
Percent of Value Placed on Selected Factors
When Employing Interscholastic Middle School Coaches

	Essential	Very Important	Important	Not Important
Knowledge of the sport	29	45	26	0
Ability to motivate athletes	42	44	13	0
Organizational skills	32	52	16	0
Effective communication with parents	38	48	13	0
Competitive spirit	48	29	21	2
First aid training	42	43	14	1
Knowledge of young adolescents	43	42	14	1

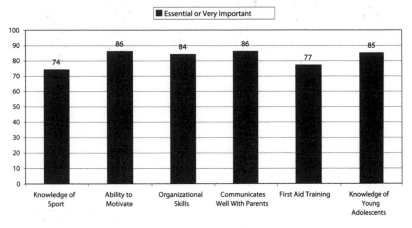

Figure 7
Importance Placed on Selected Factors When Hiring Coaches

■ Essential or Very Important

Knowledge of Sport	74
Ability to Motivate	86
Organizational Skills	84
Communicates Well With Parents	86
First Aid Training	77
Knowledge of Young Adolescents	85

In Summary

In this chapter we summarized the key findings of a national survey designed to describe existing programs and practices in middle school sports programs.

Some interesting data were found: only 58 percent of the middle level schools responding to our survey report that they have any type of intramural program in spite of the numerous calls for such activities in middle school literature. Perhaps the most surprising finding, however, was the dramatic increase in interscholastic sports programs in middle level schools, from 50 percent in 1968 to 96 percent in 2002. No doubt the contentious issues we discuss throughout this book are more prevalent given the ubiquitous nature of interscholastic sports in U.S. middle schools.

Finally, two other findings from our study are significant: 83 percent of middle level schools said they would like to have both intramural and interscholastic sports programs at their schools. Yet 75 percent of responding schools reported that their schools had no sports philosophy to guide the many decisions to be made about middle level sports.

Readers should refer back to these data as they read the following chapters. ●

3.
COMPETITIVE SPORTS ISSUES AND THE KNOWLEDGE BASE

Competition—The American Way?

Robbie, a short 12-year-old boy who has not begun to develop physically, has three goals for this basketball season. He wants to make the team and wear a uniform; he can't wait to stop at McDonald's on the way home from away games (a school tradition); and he would like to get some playing time, even though he knows he isn't very good (yet) at basketball. Robbie intuitively recognizes the purpose of middle school sports, not as a showcase for (already) gifted athletes, but as a learning laboratory for all students, just as he expects to learn from each of his courses—whether humanities, physical education, science, math, or art. Fortunately for Robbie and his classmates, teachers, administrators, and parents at Beta Middle School know that sports are an important part of the total curriculum and have set down some basic guidelines: no cuts, everyone plays, and an emphasis on learning skills, the rules of the game, and developing teamwork. High school coaches also support this approach, allowing middle school athletes to develop while keeping more students playing instead of dropping out of sports. After all, this is a middle school sports program, not professional, college, or even high school varsity.

The problems in competitive sports are widely recognized and publicized. Who hasn't heard about or seen on TV athletes fighting with each other and with fans, or reports on the use of steroids and performance-enhancing drugs, or unbelievable cases of poor sportsmanship and unprofessional behaviors by coaches? These unfortunate behaviors occur in high school, college, and professional sports. However, one should not think that such negative and dangerous occurrences are limited to those levels. One needs only to read stories in popular news magazines such as *U.S. News and World Report* (Cary, 2004) and *Newsweek* (Noonan, 2003), or in books such as *Sports in Schools* (Gerdy 2000), *Why Johnny Hates Sports* (Engh 2002), *The Cheers and the Tears* (Murphy 1999), or *Just Let the Kids Play* (Bigelow, Moroney, & Hall 2001) to understand the serious problems that exist in competitive sports for children and young adolescents.

Although the primary focus in these publications is community-based youth sports and club sports programs, the problems identified have many powerful implications for school-sponsored sports programs. These problems include, but are not limited to, coach behavior, parent behavior, low participation rates, high burnout rates, unrealistic expectations of athletes, and high injury rates. This chapter addresses some of these problem areas so that those responsible for middle school sports programs can plan and implement effective ways to offset those problems and allow young adolescents to reap the many benefits from participating in developmentally responsive interscholastic sports programs.

Competitive Sports for Young Adolescents

While the knowledge or research base concerning sports for young adolescents is limited, it is growing and substantial enough to warrant the close attention of all those responsible for the education and welfare of young adolescents. Unfortunately for young adolescents, many coaches, administrators, parents, and community members are not knowledgeable about what middle school sports could and should be; nor have they acted on the knowledge they have to take steps to make middle level sports safe, inclusive, joyful, and developmentally responsive.

The failure to make competitive middle level sports programs better reflect what is known about the realities of young adolescent development stems from a number of factors. A primary factor is a dearth of knowledge about young adolescent development (ages 10-15) in general, and especially the implications of this limited knowledge for sports participation at the middle level. Lacking knowledge, the belief that participation in sports programs is automatically good for all young adolescents regardless of the nature of that experience continues unquestioned. There are many things that can be done to build competitive sports programs based on young adolescent development, as will be pointed out in subsequent chapters. There are also model programs to study, and a number of such programs are described in this book.

An additional compounding factor that comes into play with middle level interscholastic sports is the reaction of people who are so obsessed with sports that any change is opposed without consideration—and often with anger. These adults, some of whom experience sports vicariously through the lives of young adolescents, and others who are working to establish a "winning record" are closed to any change that varies from what they perceive as the right way.

Increasing numbers of people, including recognized sports authorities, are expressing their concerns about trends in competitive sports programs both inside and outside school. For example, Metzl and Shookhoff (2002) note

> In a culture that is sports-mad, paying professional athletes vastly more than virtually anyone else, where kids pursue athletics to gain attention, respect, and scholarships, it's often difficult to remember that there is anything more important than playing and winning. (p. 77)

These authors further observe that a loss of perspective on the importance of participating in sports frequently results in undesirable outcomes, including disruption of family life, excessive stress on athletes, and the dangerous assumption on the part of those youth involved in sports that everyday rules do not apply to them.

Numerous problem areas in competitive youth sports are widely identified in the literature, including (a) win-at-all-cost coaches, (b) overzealous parents, (c) a lack of emphasis on sportsmanship, (d) high attrition rates, (e) high injury rates and other health risks, (f) the negative effects of stress and other psychological considerations, (g) a loss of perspective on sports, and (h) excessive violence (Abdal-Haqq, 2006; Bigelow, Moroney, & Hall, 2001; Carey, 2006; Engh, 2002; Kalodziej, 2006; McEwin & Dickinson, 1998; Metzl & Shookhoff, 2002; Murphy, 1999; Swaim & McEwin, 2005). These and other problematic trends and practices have detracted from the many positive aspects of sports involvement, such as increased physical activity, fun, opportunities for leadership roles, positive health habits, and enhanced self-esteem. A discussion of some of these problem areas and their implications for middle school sports programs follows.

Injuries in competitive sports

High rates of sports injuries that result from acute trauma or repetitive stress have beleaguered competitive sports programs for children and young adolescents since the beginnings of organized competitive sports. Young adolescents, usually defined as 10- to 15-year-olds, are especially susceptible to injury because of the softness of their growing bones and the relative tightness of their ligaments, tendons, and muscles. Their vulnerability is heightened by immature reflexes, an inability to recognize and evaluate risks, and underdeveloped coordination. Injury rates are highest for athletes who participate in contact sports (Haggerty & Odle, 2004). Although the vast majority of injuries to student athletes are not life-threatening, the National Athletic Trainers Association estimates that about one-third of the 7.5 million students who play interscholastic sports each year are injured, with about one-fourth of these injuries requiring treatment from physicians. Furthermore, research shows that about one-half of all injuries in organized sports could be prevented (Dillon, 2006).

One-third of the 7.5 million students who play interscholastic sports each year are injured, with about one-fourth of these injuries requiring treatment from physicians.

The high incidence of sports injuries is easily discernable by examining injury statistics. For example, a nationwide analysis of visits to hospital emergency departments conducted by the Centers for Disease Control and Prevention found that 4.3 million non-fatal sports and recreation-related injuries were treated in emergency rooms in the 12-month period ending June 2001. Although injury rates varied by age and sex, they were highest for boys 10–14. Almost 2 million youth ages 10 to 14 were treated in emergency rooms for sports and recreation injuries during the 12-month period. This number is higher than the number of youth receiving medical attention for automobile accidents and makes sports injuries a major public health concern (Centers for Disease Control, 2002; Noonan, 2003).

Those sports traditionally sponsored by schools constitute a major percentage of the sports injuries requiring emergency care. For example, during the one-year period just discussed, 144,907 10- to 14-year-olds were treated in emergency care for football injuries, 170,937 for basketball injuries, and 57,186 for soccer injuries (Centers for Disease Control, 2002). These statistics represent only injuries serious enough for emergency care and do not include visits to physicians in other settings. It is estimated that 3.5 million youth under the age of 15 require medical treatment each year for sports injuries (American Academy of Pediatrics, 2002).

Information compiled by the United States Consumer Product Safety Commission and analyzed by researchers at Loyola University Health System confirms that large numbers of participants in sports continue to be injured as

It is estimated that 3.5 million youth under the age of 15 require medical treatment each year for sports injuries.

measured by the number of visits to hospital emergency rooms. These data, which include ages 5-24, show that there were 512,213 basketball injuries, 485,669 football injuries, 418,260 soccer injuries, and 174,686 baseball injuries serious enough to require emergency room treatment in 2005. These numbers do not reflect those who sought medical attention from physicians outside hospitals (*Health News*, 2006).

Data resources on injury rates do not typically separate school-sponsored sports injuries from those occurring in non-school athletics. Therefore, questions arise regarding what percentage of these injuries occurred in organized sports versus other recreational activities, and what percentage of these injuries resulted from school-sponsored sports. Data show that of the estimated 20 to 35 million children and adolescents who participate annually in organized sport programs, about 20 percent of these youth are involved in school-based programs (Patel, 2001). Although these data do not separate injuries in the categories of school-sponsored and non-school-sponsored athletics, they make it clear that many thousands of injuries occur each year to young adolescents engaged in middle school sports programs.

Overuse injuries—repetitive micro-trauma—account for about one-half of all sports injuries at the middle and high school levels. These injuries typically occur over time with prolonged, repetitive motion or impact and range from chronic muscle strains and tendinitis to stress fractures, caused by constant overarm throwing in baseball, the pounding of feet against the ground in distance running, and the flexion and extension of the back in gymnastics. Overuse injuries tend to occur frequently in such sports as baseball, basketball, running, gymnastics, and swimming (American Academy of Pediatrics, 2002; Cassas & Cassettari-Wayhs, 2006; Dillion, 2006; Metzl & Shookhoff, 2002). The damage caused by overuse injures can be insidious because it occurs over time and may go undetected. Evidence suggests that the damage caused by overuse injuries to a growing child's hard and soft tissues can be permanent and cause problems like arthritis later in life. Repetitive coaching drills and the early specialization in a single sport cause an increase in the number of overuse injuries (Micheli, 2004). Clearly, the high injury rates of sports injuries among young adolescents are cause for alarm and must not be ignored by those responsible for middle school sports programs.

Psychological considerations

The psychological well-being of young adolescents should be considered when decisions on the nature of middle school sports are being made. Sports literature frequently focuses on such positive outcomes from participating in competitive sports as promoting socialization skills, building character, and enhancing personality development, and as "preparation for adult life" (Darst & Pangrazi, 2002; National Association for Sport and Physical Education, 2002; Seefeldt, Ewing, & Walk, 1993). These claims, at least to some extent, are based on reality. However, some authorities question the psychological readiness of children and young adolescents to cope with becoming instant successes and failures in very public ways while competing in sports activities. Engaging young adolescents in highly competitive sports before they are psychologically ready for the pressures associated with this participation can curtail the enjoyment because of regimented practices, pressures to always perform at high levels, and the exaggerated importance of winning (Metzl & Shookhoff, 2002; Swaim & McEwin, 2005).

Some authorities question the psychological readiness of children and young adolescents to cope with becoming instant successes and failures in very public ways while competing in sports activities.

Undue stress is placed on young adolescents when parents, coaches, and others have unrealistic expectations for their performances. As noted by Murphy (1999), "It is disturbing to look behind the façade and to realize that children participating in organized sport programs are sometimes unhappy, often pressured, and sometimes cruelly exploited" (p. 10). Stress can be inadvertently amplified to unhealthy levels because of direct and indirect pressures exerted by adults. These adults seem to forget that young people participating in competitive sports should be having fun and enjoying the many benefits that come from participating. For example, a national survey of 24,142 high school athletes found that 72 percent of males and females said that they would rather play on a team with a losing record than sit on the bench for a winning team (Josephson Institute of Ethics, 2004).

The widespread practice of cutting players from teams can have negative effects on the psychological development of those young adolescents who are cut. Decisions to cut are beyond the control of those young adolescents so intently wishing to be part of the team. They are based on physical maturation levels, motor competence, family issues, and the unpredictable nature of coach's judgments.

Young adolescents cut from teams often feel that they have not measured up to the expectations of adults and peers whose judgments are so important to them in determining their overall well-being (McEwin & Dickinson, 1996; Ogilvie, 1988). In some cases, being cut from sports competition leads to a decision to drop out of sports altogether. For these and related reasons, the National Association for Sport and Physical Education (2002) has recommended that a "no cut" policy should be in place at middle schools.

Attrition in sports

Although the number of youth ages 6 to 17 increased by more than seven million between 1990 and 2002, some of the most popular team sports have lost significant numbers of players. For example, the number of youth in this age group playing organized basketball has decreased from 22 million to 18 million since 1998. Soccer, after gaining in popularity from 1990 to 1998, has decreased by 1 million players since that time. Softball and baseball have also experienced decreases. The declines in participation in softball and baseball between 1990 and 2002 were 6 million and 3 million respectively (Cary, 2004). Considering that the attrition rates for competitive sports are approximately 70 percent (Engh, 2002), the decline in participation in competitive sports programs is not surprising. Since there are many potential positive outcomes associated with participating in well-planned, school-sponsored, and community-based sports programs, this decline should be a concern, and steps should be taken to reverse this trend.

The practice of involving young children in competitive sports programs is one factor leading to high attrition rates. By the time some children reach middle school, they have already played in a large numbers of games, won and lost some, traveled to away games, worn uniforms, attended sports banquets, had cheerleaders, and been awarded trophies—all of which lead some student athletes to become tired of it all and decide not to continue to participate. Even a positive experience that goes on too long can lead to young adolescents' dropping out of competitive sports (Brown, 2000).

Other factors that lead to high attrition rates include
- Lack of playing time
- The way practices are conducted
- Too much pressure
- Dislike of coaches
- A feeling of unworthiness
- Not having fun
- Harsh criticisms from coaches, parents, and team members
- Playing the same sport on multiple teams
- Too many games and practices
- The need for additional time to study.

These reasons apply to all sports, but the largest numbers of dropouts are in basketball, football, soccer, and track and field (Bigelow, 2000; Engh, 2002; Ewing & Seefelt, 1989; Holm, 1996; Rotella, Hanson & Coop, 1991; Seefeldt, Ewing & Walk, 1993; Stoker, 2000).

Typically the young adolescents eliminated or dropped out of organized sports are poor performers (e.g., later maturing boys, those who do not show enough aggression). Those individuals who most need to participate are the very ones most likely to be cut from competitive sports programs. There is also concern that these youth may turn to unhealthy options when eliminated from participation. However, gifted athletes who are forced to specialize in one sport or are placed under excessively high expectations may also drop out of sports competition (Engh, 2002; Murphy, 1999). When these youth are continually pushed to be more competitive and to participate in intense practices, they begin to burn out and sometimes lose their desire to play. This problem can also be the result of early specialization in one sport because of pressures placed on young adolescents by parents and coaches (Metzl & Shookhoff, 2002; Welsh, 2004; Wolff, 2003).

Those individuals who most need to participate are the very ones most likely to be cut from competitive sports programs.

Aspirations for scholarships and professional sports contracts

An additional problem area associated with competitive sports participation is the unrealistic expectations of parents, coaches, community members, and the young adolescents themselves regarding the prospect of obtaining college scholarships or playing professional sports. All parties concerned should be realistic about the extremely slim chances of individual young adolescents ever obtaining athletic college scholarships or becoming professional athletes. Athletes should be encouraged to reach their potential, but they should also understand that they are most unlikely to ever play at the college level or for a professional team.

According to estimates from the National Center for Educational Statistics, less than one percent of youth playing on organized sports teams receive any type of college scholarship (Ferguson, 1999). Of the one-million high school varsity football players that play each year, fewer than six percent make college teams (5.6%). This percentage includes those who play without receiving scholarships. Based on information from the National Collegiate Athletic Association, a high school senior playing football has less than a one in 1,000 chance of being drafted by a professional sports team (Metzl & Shookhoff, 2002). In basketball, approximately 475,000 fourth graders play on organized sports teams. Eighteen percent of those participating make high school teams, only .009 percent receive college scholarships, and approximately 30 will play for professional teams (.00006%). The odds are even longer in soccer because many colleges recruit players from other nations (Cary, 2004). A key message inherent in these statistical realities is the importance of helping young adolescents comprehend that although sports participation has many benefits, one's participation should not be predicated on the possibility of becoming a college or professional athlete.

Less than one percent of youth playing on organized sports teams receive any type of college scholarship.

Winning isn't everything—it's the only thing!

This oft-quoted statement by the legendary coach, Vince Lombardi, took on a life of its own; but it is uncertain if that is exactly the way he said it. Lombardi himself regretted the comment. "I wish to hell I'd never said the damned thing," he was said to have remarked shortly before his death. "I meant having a goal ... I sure as hell didn't mean for people to crush human values and morality."

—James A. Michener, *Sports in America*

Ashe County Middle School—Inclusive Sports Programs

Educators and other stakeholders at Ashe County Middle School value the benefits developmentally responsive sports participation can bring to young adolescents. The school, located in Warrensville, North Carolina, enrolls about 525 seventh and eighth grade students. Ashe Middle School is located in a mountainous area of North Carolina. The region the school serves is economically diverse, with approximately one-half of students qualifying for the free or reduced lunch program. Ashe Middle School is housed in an older school plant that was formerly a grades seven through twelve secondary school.

When Ashe Middle School was organized in 1999, a commitment was made to implement programs and practices that reflect what is known about the needs and interests of young adolescents. Results of these efforts are obvious considering the many honors the school has received including being recognized as a National School-to-Watch. This prestigious recognition is given schools that demonstrate outstanding success in the areas of academic excellence, social equity, and developmental responsiveness.

Ashe Middle School also made a commitment to provide sports experiences that are inclusive and reflect student interests. To help accomplish this goal, interscholastic, intramural, and lifetime sports are included in the sports program. Information about each of these components is provided below.

Intramural sports
- All students at Ashe Middle School participate in the intramural sports program.
- Both traditional games (e.g., basketball, volleyball) and non-traditional games (e.g., capture the flag, jail ball) are played.
- The emphasis is on participation rather than winning.
- There is an integration of core subjects in some intramural activities.
- An intramural sports scoring system is used that provides more points for being ready to play, dressing properly, showing respect, and being responsible than for winning the sports activity. For example, three points are awarded for showing respect and one for being the overall winner of the sports competition.

Lifetime sports
- Lifetime sports are also provided as part of the after-school program at Ashe Middle School.
- The only qualification for participation in this program is interest.
- Bus transportation is provided to central points in the school district so that more students can participate.
- Sports provided include golf, swimming, skiing, tennis, and other high-interest sports.

Interscholastic sports

- Two competitive sports teams are provided in baseball, basketball, football, soccer, softball, and volleyball. Plans are being made to add a third team in soccer because of the increased interest in that sport.
- Coaches select players for two-team sports in ways that balance the talent and abilities of young adolescents involved.
- Teams from two-team sports such as football and basketball play teams from other schools as well as opposing teams at Ashe Middle School.
- Sports are no-cut sports with the exception of basketball.
- With a few exceptions, cheerleading is a no-cut sport. For example, there is a no-cut cheerleading program for football.
- The interscholastic sports program emphasizes learning fundamentals and having opportunities to practice and improve skills.
- A major focus of the Ashe Middle School sports program is being a contributing member of a team rather than recognizing the performance of individuals. There are no personal trophies or other awards given, and sports ceremonies and banquets are not held.
- Championships have been won in basketball, football, and several other sports since the multiple-teams approach was established.
- After-school tutoring and time to complete homework are provided for participants when late practices are held.

● ● ●

Middle school sports as farm clubs

Many middle school competitive sports programs mirror senior high school and collegiate models rather than reflect what is known about the healthy development of all aspects of young adolescents. Too frequently, the desires and interests of coaches, family members, and even the press receive priority over the safety and welfare of youth. Unfortunately, middle school sports are viewed by some coaches, parents, and other adults as farm clubs for high school teams. For example, one respondent to the status study reported in Chapter 2 noted:

> All my players learn college plays and defenses and then
> go through a rigorous program that prepares them for
> high school. All my players are versatile. They have to
> play three or more positions. This helps them because
> they can play almost any position in high school. They are
> taught so well that the high school coaches do not have
> to re-teach.

The point of including this statement here is not to imply that all coaches see their role in this manner, but rather to demonstrate the kind of disposition that does exist in some middle school sports programs. As emphasized throughout this book, middle school interscholastic sports programs should be developmentally responsive and not viewed as farm clubs for high school athletic programs.

Other problem areas

There are many other potential problem areas associated with competitive sports that should be considered when middle school sports programs are established and then maintained in ways that benefit all participants.

One area of concern is the behavior of some parents of young athletes. Too many well-meaning parents and other adults inadvertently try to live out their own fantasies and self-expectations through the sports experiences of their children. The problem of parents' becoming obsessed with their children's achievement in sports and other areas has become so common that psychiatrists have given a name to the condition—Achievement by Proxy Syndrome (Welsh, 2004). This behavior often leads parents to pressure their children to specialize in one sport and join club sports programs that provide more intense competition, extended playing seasons, and intensive practices. Frequently, young athletes are convinced by club team coaches that if they do not join club teams and practice one sport all year, they will be left behind. Not only are these young athletes more likely to be injured more frequently, but they are also more likely to burn out or peak too early, which contributes to high attrition rates.

An additional problem area concerns the sharply increasing number of lawsuits being filed against schools, coaches, and sports equipment manufacturers for sports related injuries. In a progressively more litigious society, administrators and other school personnel are faced with the challenging task of providing for the safety of student athletes, the proper training of coaches, the maintenance of sports equipment and facilities, and related factors (Dillion, 2006; Mac, 1998). Lawsuits include not only player versus school district, but also player versus player or player versus coach or manager. Although the courts usually rule in favor of the school district and coach or manager because of the primary assumption of risk doctrine, the process is costly and time-consuming. Court cases that result in rulings in favor of the athletes tend to be those where the athlete was unaware that the alleged activity contained an inherent risk, where the coach was negligent in providing instruction, and where the sports facility did not provide a reasonably safe environment (Legal Center, 2005). In cases that rule against the school district or school personnel, the amount awarded can reach several million dollars.

There are also legal implications concerning gender issues and interscholastic sports participation. Although significant progress has been made regarding females' participating in interscholastic sports since the enactment of Title IX of the Educational Amendments in 1972, which prohibits gender discrimination in institutions that receive federal funds, many experts say that gender discrimination at the elementary, middle, and high school levels continues to be a nationwide problem. Care should be taken to make sure that interscholastic sports provide equal opportunities for boys and girls.

Lawsuits are also filed for reasons other than physical injury, and no one associated with sports is immune from the threat of a lawsuit. Middle schools should have management risk plans and take all precautions to ensure that competitive sports programs are fairly organized and supervised and as safe as possible for participants.

In Summary

This chapter is not meant to point out the negative aspects of competitive sports in the school and community so that interscholastic sports programs will be discredited or eliminated. Rather, we believe it is important that the problems be recognized if they are to be solved and interscholastic sports can be made developmentally responsive.

Interscholastic competitive sports programs are neither inherently good nor evil. Clearly, it is the quality of those programs that makes the difference. There are many actions that can be taken to help ensure that middle school interscholastic sports are both safe and developmentally responsive, and they will be addressed later in this book. The examples of programs from middle schools included will help readers better comprehend the types of interscholastic sports programs that lead to rewarding athletic experiences for young adolescents and those who work with them. Young adolescents who participate in interscholastic sports programs have no role in deciding the way the programs operate; they are wholly dependent on adults to design and operate them. ●

4.
DEVELOPMENTALLY RESPONSIVE MIDDLE LEVEL SPORTS PROGRAMS

He loves sports, is rather mediocre at most of them, but likes to play. Will there be a place for him in middle school athletics—just for fun and not because of great skill? —Parents of a sixth grader

In the early days of the movement from junior high schools to middle schools, much of the literature regarded intramural sports programs as most appropriate for young adolescents, while interscholastic sports were considered too dangerous and developmentally inappropriate to be part of the middle school program.

For instance, a 1978 article in *Middle School Journal* opened with these three sentences:

> *Many communities are taking a new look at the educational programs for their middle-school-aged learners. As a result, one of the programs that has been common in junior high schools, interscholastic sports, is now being questioned seriously. Proponents of the middle school are challenging programs of interscholastic sports on the grounds that this kind of activity is not consistent with what is known about the emotional and physical needs of these youngsters.* (Romano & Timmers, p. 3)

But it was not just middle school educators who were raising questions about the appropriateness of interscholastic sports for young adolescents. Back in 1952, a committee of representatives from five major organizations proclaimed, "Interscholastic competition of a varsity pattern is definitely disapproved for children below the ninth grade" (p. 3).

When the characteristics of proposed middle schools were set forth in the literature, intramural sports programs then were usually included along with such features as interdisciplinary team organization, flexible scheduling, and teacher advisory programs. Typically, intramural sports programs were listed as part of the middle school concept, while interscholastic sports were not (Georgiady, Riegle, & Romano, 1973; Hansen & Hearn, 1971; Vars, 1965).

Middle school sports in the early years

Many early middle schools intentionally excluded interscholastic sports from their programs. Alexander (1968) conducted a national survey of middle schools and found that only about one-half (52%) of middle schools had interscholastic sports programs and over one-half (57%) had intramural programs (p. 20). As noted previously, this has now changed rather dramatically, with 96 percent of middle schools having interscholastic programs in one or more sports.

As the middle school movement grew, its identity began to be defined by a set of beliefs rather than a loosely connected list of educational components or characteristics. The belief statements listed in Chapter 1 represent the conceptual framework currently accepted by most educators as defining middle school education (NMSA, 2003). The underlying concept that binds these belief statements together is that a middle level educational program should be designed with all its features in keeping with the nature and needs of young adolescents. Thus the ultimate measure of how effective middle schools are is not whether they possess particular programmatic components but whether the features of the schools are developmentally appropriate for young adolescents.

The ultimate measure of how effective middle schools are is not whether they possess particular programmatic components but whether the features of the schools are developmentally appropriate for young adolescents.

With this more conceptual approach to the middle school movement, it is important for middle level schools to have developmentally responsive intramural and interscholastic sports programs rather than eliminate or fail to establish one or the other of these programs. Both kinds of sports programs are needed to serve young adolescents well— when they are properly planned and implemented in ways that reflect the physical, social, and emotional characteristics of young adolescents.

Intramural sports programs

With interscholastic sports programs now nearly universal in middle schools, it is obvious how widespread is the belief that competitive sports are good for young adolescents. Intramurals, however, receive much more limited support. While few negative views toward intramurals are ever voiced, the gung ho attitude that supports interscholastic programs is missing. When respondents in the national survey were asked whether they believed intramural sports should be offered in middle schools, 83 percent stated that intramurals should be offered along with interscholastic sports. An additional six percent believed that only intramural sports should be provided. The large difference between beliefs about the importance of intramural sports and actual implementation of those programs constitutes a very large discrepancy. Major reasons quality middle level intramural programs are not implemented in most middle schools include

- Pressures from senior high school coaches to maintain programs that prepare athletes for varsity sports participation.
- Pressures from parents and community members to give interscholastic sports high priority.
- Difficulties with scheduling intramural sports.
- Lack of adequate coaches for intramurals.
- Complications caused by having a small student population.
- Difficulties caused by limited funding.
- A widespread lack of understanding by educators and others regarding the importance of intramural sports.

Interscholastic sports programs

A major challenge in implementing developmentally responsive middle school interscholastic programs is the presence of multiple external influences that impact such programs, ones that do not significantly impact intramural programs. Once sports competition extends beyond an individual school and school district, some control is lost. For example, when middle level sports programs are part of a league, the rules and practices of that league, which may not be a good match for the sports philosophy of an individual school, take priority. One of the authors experienced this phenomenon when he was principal of a middle school that was part of an eight-school league of middle schools from different school districts. A proposal was made that league rules be changed so that more young adolescents could play in games. This proposal failed because many league participants felt strongly that they should play only their best players so that they would have a better chance of winning. Interestingly, many who voted no on the proposal agreed with the proposal but feared the lack of support they would receive from parents and other community members. The author and coaches at his school then had to make a decision about whether to continue giving all athletes opportunities to play or follow the practices of the other league teams by playing only the best-performing players. The choice was made to continue to play as many athletes as possible in every game. Although the team did not often have a winning season, it was competitive and won its share of games. Unfortunately, many opponents chose to play their best players for whole games while they ran up the scores and left their other players on the bench. The goal of allowing as many young adolescents as possible to play and gain the benefits of sports participation is a low priority with most adults while the *win-at-all-costs* attitude continues to prevail.

The authors have no easy answers for ways to develop and maintain interscholastic sports programs that are focused on the characteristics and needs of young adolescents, but it is important to continue to strive to get rules and procedures changed in appropriate ways. When league rules are not changed, those responsible for individual teams should find ways to participate and still retain practices that best reflect the needs and interests of their students. This task will not be simple or without controversy. The influence of high school and college athletic programs is pervasive. Coaches and parents must fully understand and support the goals and practices of developmentally responsive sports programs so that they can lend their support to needed changes. When possible, leagues should be formed that involve multiple schools from the same school district, as it is easier to modify practices with like-minded schools within a single school district.

Once middle schools are committed to interscholastic programs focused on tenets that make them developmentally responsive for young adolescents and have accepted the reality that developing and maintaining these programs will be challenging, strategies to accomplish the goals should be designed and implemented. Many of the resulting decisions will be questioned by those who do not understand or support the proposed changes. The information presented in this book should arm those committed to reforming interscholastic sports programs.

Plainfield Community Middle School—Widespread Opportunities

Plainfield Community Middle School (PCMS), in Plainfield, Indiana, enrolls almost 1,000 students. The building was designed to accommodate teaming and wide student participation. During the development of PCMS, a learn-by-doing philosophy was adopted with a commitment to establish developmentally appropriate curricular and cocurricular activities. This concept, referred to at PCMS as *widespread opportunity*, provides a wide assortment of activities based solely on student interest. Young adolescents are encouraged to engage in many activities as long as that participation does not diminish academic performance. This policy applies to academics and cocurricular programs as well as to interscholastic sports.

The rationale for increasing student participation has not diminished the quality of educational experiences or interscholastic sports programs. PCMS has received the Four Star School Award for academic achievement, the state's highest award, for 10 consecutive years. Many other awards for academic achievement have also been received. The PCMS *widespread participation* program has also been featured in numerous newspaper and magazine articles including the *New York Times, Sports Illustrated*, and *People*, as well as on radio stations and local and national television.

Intramural sports
- All students are eligible to participate in the intramural sports program.
- Students participate in volleyball or basketball during the last 30 minutes of their lunch periods.
- Students select their own intramural teams.
- In volleyball, the first team to score five points wins, with the winning team staying on the court until it loses. The use of two courts allows four teams to play at one time.
- In basketball, the first team to score three buckets wins, with shots being taken from behind the three-point line. As in volleyball, the winning team stays on the floor until it loses.
- Knock-out, another basketball game involving long and short shots, is a competition that is very popular with students.

Interscholastic sports
Some features of the interscholastic and intramural sports programs at Plainfield Community Middle School are provided below:
- A no-cut policy has been instituted for sports that are not restricted by facility limitations: cross-country, football, wrestling, swimming, track, and cheerleading.
- Dual scheduling of A and B games gives student athletes opportunities to participate in interscholastic contests regardless of their ability levels.
- Coaches emphasize continual improvement over winning.
- Widespread participation promotes teamwork skills.
- Track teams have intra-squad meets for participants who are unable to compete in away meets due to participation limits set by host schools. Home events allow athletes to sign up for open events in addition to those assigned by coaches.
- Every home wrestling and swimming contest gives every athlete the opportunity to compete in at least one match.

● ● ●

Plainfield Community Middle School

Phone: 317.838.3966

http://schools .publicschoolreport .com/IndianaPlainfield/PlainfieldComMiddleSch.html

Participation-based sports programs

Three major factors influence the number of athletes who can participate in middle school sports—staffing, facilities, and funding. The quality and safety of middle level sports programs depend on having adequate space, equipment, and supervision. When qualified coaches cannot be found on the school staff, one solution is to hire persons outside the school. The advantages and disadvantages of this practice are discussed in the next chapter. The lack of suitable sports facilities offers other challenges. Sometimes these problems can be solved by using facilities in local elementary schools or local recreational facilities. The best way to significantly increase participation, however, is to establish interscholastic sports combined with comprehensive intramurals.

All middle level students, including those involved in interscholastic sports programs, should participate in intramural sports programs. To help ensure that interscholastic athletes do not dominate intramural programs, they should be distributed across the intramural teams. A modification of this policy might be not to allow varsity athletes to compete in the same sport in intramurals as they do in interscholastics. This helps to make the intramural program school-wide so that everyone understands that intramurals are equally as important as interscholastics. Not allowing varsity players to participate in intramural sports at all gives the appearance that intramurals are designed only for those who are not successful enough to make the real teams.

An additional way to make middle level sports programs safe and inclusive is to adopt modified rules for some sports, such as including playing an extra quarter with rotating teams and limiting the number of times any one athlete can play. Fortunately, allowing many athletes to play is not a problem in sports such as track and field events.

With creative ideas and a sincere desire to have as many young adolescents as possible participate, much can be accomplished. For example, Bob Bigelow, former professional basketball star and co-author of *Just Let Them Play* (Bigelow, Moroney, & Hall, 2001), suggests that football fields be divided into halves so that two games can be played at the same time. He also recommends that two basketball games be played at the same time using the side baskets on basketball courts with twice as many young people participating. The same thing can be done for volleyball and possibly other sports.

Strong intramural and interscholastic sports programs help fulfill the vision of authentic middle schools dedicated to serving the needs and interests of all young adolescents. However, when middle schools have viable intramural and interscholastic programs and still have difficulty providing all middle level students opportunities to participate, cooperative agreements may be worked out with city recreation departments and club sports programs to help accommodate some students. Caution should be exercised, however,

All middle level students, including those involved in interscholastic sports programs, should participate in intramural sports programs.

about working with and supporting outside sports programs, since some of these programs do not attempt to make accommodations for the needs, interests, and safety of young adolescents.

To operate a middle school sports program, two basic criteria must be met: adequate supervision and provisions to ensure safety. Finding the funds to meet these criteria is a major problem for many middle schools. Some school districts charge a fee for participating—pay to play. Although this may be deemed necessary in some locations, this practice should be used only as a last resort. Charging students to play for their schools is a barrier to wide participation.

An additional barrier is the common policy of cutting players from teams. This concern was expressed by respondents in the authors' national survey. The most frequent response to the question, *If you could change one thing about your interscholastic sports program, what would it be?* was "I would have a no-cuts policy." At this level, young adolescents wishing to participate in sports should not be cut any more than they should be eliminated from academic programs. Every attempt should be made to provide students with opportunities to participate in meaningful ways. Educators have an obligation to keep young adolescents involved in sports and nurture them while they are developing. For many if not most youth, the middle grades are their last opportunity to gain the benefits of being part of a team under the tutelage of a coach.

Modification of rules

In middle schools where interscholastic sports programs emulate senior high programs, they tend to use the same rules and policies. Likewise, senior high schools likely use the rules and regulations of college sports. Such practices continue to be widely accepted despite the wide discrepancies among the various developmental age groups. Too often 10- to 15-year-olds are playing under rules designed for adult athletes!

This serious mismatch of practices begs for change. If rules and regulations governing middle school sports programs are to be developmentally responsive, they must be specifically designed for young adolescents. When rules are so designed, they will help middle school athletes build the skills they need to participate successfully in various sports.

Rules designed for middle level sports make changes that
• Allow more athletes to participate (e.g., no-cut policies; limited playing time for individuals).

• Ensure athletes' safety (e.g., no metal spikes; no blitzing in football; weight class modifications in wrestling; no pole vaulting in track).

• Accommodate the skill and conditioning levels of young adolescents (e.g., no pressing in basketball; using smaller basketballs; pitching distance in baseball; adjusting the size of playing fields; five hits per side in volleyball; no kickoffs in football; coaches allowed on field in football; shorter distances in track and cross-country; use of a smaller shot in track).

• De-emphasize high stakes competition by applying the mercy rule when one team gets too far ahead; clearing the score every quarter; limiting the number of innings pitched; limiting the number of games and other competitions during a season.

The old adage that the best way to prepare for a game is to practice it may not always apply to middle school sports. In fact, good coaches know you do not play under strict game conditions when you are trying to prepare for a game. Emulating high school sports programs may be counterproductive, not only at the middle school level, but even later in high school for young adolescents. It is more productive to adapt the sports program to fit the athletes rather than trying to fit young adolescent athletes to the program.

Practices

One of the things student athletes rate as valuable in their athletic experience is attending practices (Schenkenfelder, 2000). However, one of the main causes for students' dropping out of sports is the fact that practices are not fun and are often cited as boring (Brown, 2000; Stoker, 2000). This disconnect between the participation and enjoyment that young adolescents want to experience and what they experience is an example of how those responsible for sports programs have not made the system fit the students, but rather have instituted practices that discourage athletes from future participation in sports.

Although conditioning is important for young adolescents, teaching skills and the enjoyment of the game are equally important. Activities during practices should be a mix of conditioning, teaching skills, and just having fun. Practices should actively involve all athletes rather than have some sit while others dominate the practice time. Drills should allow the more talented athletes to work together, but there should also be drills that allow the less talented athletes to work with the more talented athletes, rather than completely segregating the two groups. Doing so builds a sense of total team spirit and may even help the coaches discover talents in athletes which might not have surfaced if they had not been given opportunities to compete at higher levels. For example, rather than run a series of windsprints with all the athletes at the same time, a coach might divide the team into groups of three, spread the talent out among the groups, and run relays. This way all athletes receive the same conditioning, the activity remains competitive, and all are members of a team.

To assume that all young adolescents have short attention spans, as is commonly done, may be generally accurate, but this short attention span is often overinterpreted. Young adolescents have varying attention spans, but when they are engaged in something they like, they can stay with it for an hour or more. The real challenge becomes one of channeling their energies in the directions they need and want to go.

Practices and drills during practices should be shorter and more intense, should focus on skills, involve all students, and indeed, be enjoyable. An extended period devoted to conditioning should be limited and adapted to the various skill and conditioning levels of the athletes. A coach might not have some athletes do as many repetitions of a drill as others who are in better condition. The goal is ensuring that athletes are in good enough condition to safely compete in sports.

Length of season and sports specialization

Early adolescence should be a time for youth to explore their talents and interests both in classrooms and on the playing fields. Unfortunately, our society seems to be forcing young persons to specialize intellectually and athletically at earlier and earlier ages. This results in specializing early in a single sport to the exclusion of other sports (Ferguson, 1999; Wolff, 2003). It appears that the three-letter athlete in high school may become a thing of the past except in small schools. To be an elite high school athlete, specialization in that sport is now almost a necessity requiring year-round commitment—with one result being significant increases in injury rates (Micheli, 2004).

One way to help young adolescents have a more well-rounded sports experience in middle school is to have shorter seasons that do not overlap. This gives athletes opportunities to participate in multiple sports and perhaps discover talents and interests they did not know they had. With shorter seasons, coaches will need to conserve time by combining conditioning and teaching skills while still making the season enjoyable. Shorter seasons also may help solve the coaching shortage since more than one sport can be coached by an individual. Eliminating tournaments and end-of-season competitions is one way to shorten the seasons. In tournaments, schools playing for championships typically become more competitive and less participation based. Middle schools that have maintained participation-based programs during the season may be pushed to allow only a few of their best athletes to play during tournaments.

It is better for all schools involved if the seasons end without tournaments. Eliminating tournaments saves time and places the emphasis on learning skills and enjoying participation rather than on winning championships. With tournaments, and especially championship tournaments, all teams end up feeling like losers except the one team that wins. This is also the case in individual-based competitions. Despite the popularity among adults of having one championship winner, school-sponsored interscholastic sports programs need to find ways to deemphasize the importance of winning and help young adolescents understand the significance of improving their individual performance while enjoying their sports participation.

Club and community sports programs

Club and community sports are becoming more and more popular, having developed multi-level teams with sports like soccer and swimming. Frequently these sports programs, especially club teams, include frequent practices, extensive travel, and intense competition. Community-based sports programs such as Little League provide additional sports participation options for students but create the possibilities that young adolescents will have to participate in a single school-sponsored and a community-sponsored sport at the same time.

Some middle schools guard against students' participating in the same school-sponsored and community-sponsored sport by creating policies that govern participation. In the authors' national survey, 69 percent of middle level schools reported that they allow athletes to compete in club and community sports while still participating in school sports, 15 percent allowed athletes to compete in outside-school sports if it was not the same sport, and only 11 percent allowed athletes to compete in outside-school sports when they were also playing in that same sport at school. When schools were asked if club and community sports affected their sports programs, 62 percent indicated this had not had any major effect, while 16 percent believed that club and community sports had actually increased participation in their sports programs.

Although the survey indicates that the majority of respondents did not view club and community sports as problems, difficulties do arise. For instance, when younger children specialize in one sport, they then have to make a decision upon entering middle school about whether to participate in school-sponsored sports or to limit their participation to community or club sports. This is already occurring at senior high school levels, where athletes practice with their club teams and only represent their school in games or other competitions. Caution should be taken when athletes participate in club and community sports at the same time they are participating in middle school sports. This practice may lead young adolescents to become emotionally and physically overextended, may increase the chances for stress fractures and tendinitis, and may contribute to sports attrition at early ages (Micheli, 2004).

Another difficulty associated with overspecialization at young ages is that it does not provide youth with the opportunity to explore other sports they might enjoy and in which they might excel as they become more mature. This is not to say that young adolescents should never be allowed to participate in community or club sports while playing for a school team. However, care should be taken to ensure that the student, his or her coaches, parents, and other adults make the best decision for each individual rather than one based on adult desires to see young athletes succeed in sports performances.

Eligibility issues
Ninety percent of schools responding in the national survey indicated that their interscholastic sports programs included formal eligibility policies. There are generally two factors that determine eligibility: academic record and behavior. Most middle schools have clearly stated

rules regarding eligibility and the consequences if the athlete fails to comply with them. The problem is that most eligibility systems stop there, leaving some athletes on their own to figure out how to become eligible again if they are denied permission to participate. Unfortunately, many young adolescents who find themselves in this situation do not seek out adults who might help them find solutions. This results not only in the loss of prospective athletes, but may also mean that the individuals concerned give up on becoming more successful in their academics or being concerned with positive behaviors.

Good middle schools take the extra step of helping students get back on track by providing interventions to assist them. Middle schools with advocacy programs, where every student is known well by at least one adult, use this connection to regain eligibility. Another approach is to have ineligible athletes report to practice, but instead of practicing use the time to catch up on academic work. This latter approach works if athletes are simply behind on assignments. When athletes are ineligible because they need extra help in understanding a subject, tutoring and other forms of assistance should be provided.

Assistance for athletes who are ineligible for behavioral reasons will depend on the severity of the behaviors, with consequences ranging from not being able to play for a predetermined number of competitions to being suspended for entire seasons. As in any discipline system, the punishment should fit the behavior; and steps should be taken to help individuals improve. All middle schools should continually review their eligibility policies to make sure they allow for some flexibility and are not a one-size-fits-all plan. Eligibility policies should be equitable and rigorous enough to benefit the academic achievement and overall behavior of all individuals affected by the policies.

Awards and recognitions

Middle level students desire to succeed and be recognized for achievements in meaningful ways. While successful athletes and teams should be recognized, this should be done in a way that acknowledges achievement but does not place the majority of young adolescents in the position of feeling unsuccessful. Awards and recognitions at the middle level should focus on recognizing the efforts of all participants without young adolescents feeling undue pressures from peers, coaches, and parents to be individually recognized.

Recognizing a team's success generally includes all athletes. Recognition of individuals should be more direct and personal. This will require coaches to look for ways to recognize athletes for accomplishments other than scoring goals in soccer, hitting home runs, or taking multiple first places in track competitions. Although athletes who excel should be recognized, those who have shown improvement or who are putting forth an extra effort need as much encouragement, if not more. Sometimes making significant improvement is as worthy of recognition as scoring a goal. Likewise, formal and public recognition of efforts and improvement should be included at award ceremonies and in other venues. Informal recognition and encouragement of both coaches and all athletes are equally important in developmentally responsive sports programs. As with other components of middle level sports programs, appropriate and meaningful recognitions can provide positive experiences for young adolescents when carried out with an understanding of this age group.

In Summary

The recommendations presented in this chapter are intended to guide sports programs that are specifically developed for middle school students. The challenges of these recommendations lie not in questions about whether they should be implemented, but rather for their use in reconceptualizing traditional sports programs to reflect the needs, interests, and safety of young adolescents. This task is complex and needs support from many stakeholders to be successful. For those involved in well-entrenched interscholastic sports programs that mimic high school and college sports, the challenge will be particularly difficult. However, there are a growing number of middle schools that have found ways to implement many, if not all, of these recommendations. ●

5.
COACHING AND DIRECTING MIDDLE LEVEL SPORTS PROGRAMS

Good coaches know their players not just as athletes but as youngsters with a wide range of other interests and talents.
—Kelly Hill, American Sport Education Program

N o doubt about it, the most critical element in successful, developmentally responsive middle level interscholastic sports programs are qualified coaches, perhaps even more important at this level than in high school. In addition, it is also crucial to have qualified professionals to administer and implement successful middle level intramural sports programs. This chapter explores topics related to coaching interscholastic sports and administering intramural programs, with special emphasis on the characteristics of successful coaches and directors of middle level intramural programs. No matter what the configuration of the sports program, middle school sports programs must be staffed by qualified adults who understand and appreciate the realities of working with young adolescents.

Certainly coaches are the key to making the athletic experiences of young adolescents appropriate, positive, and educational. However, this is not easy given the difficulty of finding highly qualified coaches for any level of schooling—particularly at the middle school level. Sixty-one percent of respondents in the authors' national study agreed or strongly agreed that finding coaches who are knowledgeable about young adolescent development is difficult.

Teachers as coaches
Most middle level coaching positions are filled by teachers who assume coaching duties in addition to their instructional responsibilities. Although only 23 percent of respondents to the middle school sports

survey reported that willingness to coach was a major factor in hiring teachers, in the majority (51%) of the responding schools over 90 percent of the coaches were certified teachers. Clearly, a close relationship exists between coaching positions and certified teachers.

In some cases, new teachers accept coaching positions only because they are seeking a teaching position and agreeing to coach is a condition of employment. Some are well qualified and excited about the opportunity to coach. However, many novice teachers lack sufficient knowledge about young adolescent development and the sports they will be coaching to be truly qualified for the coaching positions they accept.

There are built-in risks when hiring new teachers for coaching positions even when they are qualified. The challenges beginning teachers face during their first years are difficult enough without the added responsibility of coaching assignments. To compound the problem, novice teachers are often assigned a heavy teaching load with low-ability or overcrowded classes, or multiple preparations. Additionally, these novice teacher-coaches may be asked to coach multiple sports or even be the head coach of a sport that draws outside pressures from parents and community members. Placing new teachers in such a situation often results in their inability to give full efforts to either teaching or coaching,

When new teachers are assigned coaching duties, their teaching responsibilities should be considered and their loads adjusted.

resulting in a loss of confidence and added stress that discourages them from coaching and teaching. This is not to say that teachers should not also be coaches, but rather to caution against the use of teachers, especially novice ones, who are not qualified to coach or who do not really wish to do so. When new teachers are assigned coaching duties, their teaching responsibilities should be carefully considered and their loads adjusted.

Coaching responsibilities for novices should also be assigned so that no undue internal or external pressures are involved. Many schools help new teachers in their first year by assigning mentors—a practice that could be used for new coaches. When the adjustment of teaching and coaching responsibilities is not possible, administrators should be forthright with new teachers as to what the teaching and coaching responsibilities will require. Well-qualified teachers who also coach need the support of administrators and others responsible for the sports programs. Simply being qualified does not guarantee success. Coaches still need support.

Many middle level coaches participated in athletics at the high school and college levels. Therefore, they may know the sport they coach from a participant's point of view, but may not have much experience with young adolescents or the middle school concept. This may lead to coaching that focuses on winning and practices that do not take into consideration the need to be developmentally responsive.

Coaches who have never coached at the middle level may be in for a rude awakening when they discover that the students on the seventh-grade boys' basketball team are not as committed to the game as they were when they participated in high school or college sports. It may prove frustrating when young adolescents are unable to pick up the most fundamental skills, even when the coach has demonstrated them several times. New coaches may not realize that losing a game is devastating to young adolescents—but only until they are on the bus ready to go back to school. This is very different from the past experiences of many coaches, who worried about lost games for days or even months afterward. In some cases, the resulting frustration leads to coaches' displaying poor sportsmanship. However, some greatly enjoy coaching this age group and understand that teaching is a primary purpose of coaching young adolescents.

Additional factors associated with qualified middle level coaching
Another reason why it is difficult to find and retain highly qualified middle level coaches is the limited compensation most receive for long hours and hard work. Although there are greater expectations and pressures at the high school level, the time commitment and responsibilities are still substantially the same. Middle school coaches put in as much time as high school coaches, but are paid significantly less. Should there be parity between the two levels of schooling?

> *Middle school coaches put in as much time as high school coaches, but are paid significantly less.*

The nature of coaching at the middle level has changed in recent years. In the past it was under the direction of high school coaches who were primarily interested in posting winning seasons and championship teams. Middle level coaches were expected to introduce young athletes to organized sports and help them build the necessary skills to compete successfully at the high school level. However, as with other things in our educational system and society, expectations and responsibilities have been pushed further down the K-12 continuum. This change of focus may discourage some people from coaching because they wish to avoid the stress brought about by this new set of expectations. The rewards of coaching young adolescents may have been diminished by the pressure to win so prevalent in many communities.

Today, children participate in organized sports as early as preschool and come to the middle level having already experienced sports activities only available to older youth in the past. Instead of sixth or seventh graders having a coach for the first time, they may have already played multiple sports and had several coaches. As a result, many young adolescents come to middle schools expecting to participate in highly competitive interscholastic sports. These expectations are frequently reflected in the attitudes and expectations of their parents.

The way middle level sports has been redefined over the last two or three decades makes it difficult for coaches to maintain competitive sports models that are developmentally responsive, inclusive, as safe as possible, and fun for participants. This situation is likely a contributing factor to the shortage of qualified middle level coaches.

Part-time middle level coaches

One solution to the shortage of middle level coaches is the practice of employing part-time coaches from outside the school faculty. However, this is typically a short-term fix. For example, employing college students means that in one or two years they will graduate and move on. One of the biggest drawbacks and dangers of hiring outside coaches, including those available in the community, is that most have no formal preparation for coaching. They may possess knowledge of a sport's tactical and technical aspects but may have a very limited understanding of developmentally responsive middle level interscholastic sports. An additional disadvantage is that these coaches do not have daily contact with young adolescents and find it difficult to get to know the students they coach. Whenever possible, middle school coaches should be faculty members at the middle school where they coach.

Whenever possible, middle school coaches should be faculty members at the middle school where they coach.

The difficulty of securing qualified coaches, however, cannot be allowed to stifle efforts to find these coaches and provide them with the support and encouragement they need to continue to serve young adolescents well. Making both current and prospective middle school coaches, as well as those responsible for administering sports programs, aware of appropriate coaching practices is a first step toward creating middle school sports programs that are responsive to the needs of all young adolescent athletes.

Characteristics of effective intramural directors and interscholastic coaches

Like effective teachers, effective coaches and administrators of middle level intramural sports programs should (a) be knowledgeable about the developmental characteristics of young adolescents; (b) value working with them; (c) be well-grounded in the academic subjects they teach and the sports they coach; and (d) possess the ability to share that knowledge and understanding in ways that are motivating and developmentally appropriate for the students they teach and coach. Responses to the national survey tend to affirm that these characteristics are essential elements for successful middle level coaching. Although a competitive spirit (48%) was rated as the most essential characteristic of a middle school coach, knowledge of young adolescents (42%) and ability to motivate (42%) were also rated as essential. Surprisingly, knowledge of the sport was rated essential by only 29 percent of the respondents.

Excellent examples of the proper and improper roles of middle level interscholastic sports coaches are provided in *Sports Done Right* (University of Maine, 2005). This report notes that effective middle school coaches "promote the connection between sports and academic learning, sports and character development, and sports and lifelong learning" and "are sensitive to the fact that different approaches will be needed for different individuals according to their needs and backgrounds, including their age, gender, size, and culture" (p. 20). Examples are also provided of inappropriate roles that should be avoided by middle level coaches, such as failing to understand that they are first and foremost teachers, using the win-at-all-costs philosophy, and being autocratic and modeling poor sportsmanship (p. 21). The authors support those principles and offer the following additions for consideration:

- *Effective middle level coaches avoid comparing performances among young adolescent athletes.* When coaching young adolescents, it is important not to compare one athlete to another, for there is a wide difference in physical abilities at this age. By comparing, or even using more talented athletes as examples for their performances, coaches may discourage less talented or physically immature athletes rather than inspiring them to continue to improve. Particularly at the middle level, coaches should keep in mind that the athletes they work with are still developing and will not be able to maximize their athletic talent now. It can be discouraging for less physically mature young adolescents who are putting forth maximum effort to be continually reminded by the coach that they have less talent than others on the team. Rather than compare one athlete to another, it is more productive for coaches to focus on the progress individuals are making.

- *Effective middle level coaches avoid using sarcasm or harsh criticism.* Coaches should be careful not to criticize or use sarcasm with this age group, for young adolescents are especially vulnerable to criticism. Well-meaning suggestions, even ones meant to be humorous, may be taken to heart in negative ways not intended. Most young adolescents are still primarily concrete thinkers, and they often interpret things very literally. Therefore, when coaches say something that is sarcastic, it is often taken literally. Pointing out and correcting imperfections in an athlete's game or performance is an essential part of coaching, but at the middle level this should be done in a positive manner.

- *Effective middle level coaches understand that young adolescents often act impulsively.* This happens on the playing field as well as in other life experiences and can be frustrating to coaches as well as to other adults. Sports participation can help young adolescents learn about actions and consequences in positive ways if coaches refrain from getting angry and understand the developmental stages of those they are coaching. It does little good to become angry and criticize young adolescents for something they do impulsively. To add to the frustration of coaching at this level, the same behavior may occur more than one time. Effective coaches correct inappropriate behaviors in ways that do not demean student athletes and look for authentic ways to praise positive behaviors and performances on the playing fields. Being positive and encouraging are critical aspects of successful middle school coaching.

- *Effective middle level coaches always exhibit ethical behavior.* Middle level coaches are role models for the athletes they coach and for others who attend sports competitions. Every sport has rules and regulations that are designed to make the sport fair for everyone. However, when the desire to win becomes more important than participation in the sport itself, bending or breaking the rules becomes tempting. Although breaking rules is unethical for many reasons, it can be especially destructive for young adolescents to receive a message that cheating is acceptable as long as victory is achieved. During this formative time when they are discovering who they are, it is critical that young adolescents associate with role models who are ethical. Middle school coaches' responsibilities go well beyond teaching the technical aspects of sports and include teaching young adolescents, playing by the rules, demonstrating good sportsmanship, and winning and losing gracefully.

- *Effective middle level coaches always maintain their composure and express their enthusiasm in appropriate ways.* There is a difference between being excited or demonstrative and letting your emotions get out of control. Coaches who lose their tempers and yell when they do not like a call made on the field, sometimes even using profanity, set a very bad example for young adolescents. The same poor behavior can be demonstrated when coaches yell at players when they do not perform up to expectations. Such negative actions by coaches are a sign that they are putting their emotions before the welfare of the youngsters they coach. Middle school coaches should constantly ask themselves, "Are my actions on the playing field and during practice self-promoting, or are they for the good of the individuals I coach?"

- *Effective middle level coaches need to avoid becoming so wrapped up in the game that they forget that it is primarily about the young adolescents and not themselves.* An effective coach is able to enjoy the victories while allowing the athletes to be center stage. It is best when a team wins a tournament that the players, and not the coach, accept the trophy and carry it around. There are subtle ways for a coach to enjoy the excitement of sports while allowing the athletes to feel the glory. For instance, when athletes do something out of the ordinary, instead of the coach being the first to congratulate them, conscientious coaches might encourage fellow teammates to offer their congratulations first.

Effective middle level coaches keep winning in proper perspective.

- *Effective middle level coaches keep winning in proper perspective.* This does not mean that winning is not important, but teaching the skills involved in a sport to all the athletes and making sure that they have opportunities to participate should be valued over the need to win. Athletics by their very nature are competitive.

- *Effective middle level coaches spend time working with all team members.* Middle school coaches should work intently with *all* participants rather than predominantly with a select few. It can be tempting for coaches to spend most of their time and energy on the most talented athletes to the detriment of other less mature or skilled athletes. Less talented athletes will likely have less participation time during competitions but should not receive less attention and assistance during practice. Good coaches receive personal satisfaction from seeing the success of all athletes. In developmentally responsive middle schools, all young adolescents must be provided with multiple opportunities to learn and to participate to the best of their abilities.

- *Effective middle level coaches work well with parents.* The ability to communicate well with parents and other family members is another skill that effective coaches possess. They should work closely with family members to establish roles that are supportive rather than adversarial. It should be recognized that often parents have been involved with competitive sports for many years and have expectations based on their experiences. Coaches need to help these parents and other stakeholders understand the distinctive goals and objectives of middle school sports so that as many young adolescents as possible can participate in competitive athletics in safe, caring, and inclusive environments.

There are many successful middle school coaches who possess the essential characteristics discussed in this section. If middle school sports are to become more than feeder systems for senior high schools, these coaches need to take the initiative and promote programs that are developmentally responsive. When this occurs, more young adolescents will have positive experiences in intramural and interscholastic sports programs.

Coaches play a special role in the lives of young adolescents.

Barren County Middle School—Coaches as Mentors

Barren County Middle School, located in Glasgow, Kentucky, houses approximately 650 students enrolled in grades seven and eight. The school has received widespread recognition for its success, including being selected as one of the first Schools-to-Watch in the nation.

The Barren County Middle School athletic program

The ultimate goal of the Barren County Middle School athletic program is to enable all young adolescents to reach their greatest potential as individuals, as members of a team, and as members of the community. Coaches serve as mentors for students as they challenge them to continually pursue the *habits of champions* and become leaders on the playing fields as well as in their classrooms and beyond. Interscholastic sports offered at BCMS are baseball, basketball, cheerleading, cross-country, football, and golf. Because only limited numbers of young adolescents are selected for varsity competition, educators at BCMS extend opportunities for participation through the intramural sports program. Intramural sports offered include tennis, soccer, softball, swimming, and track.

The role of coaches

The important role of coaches is recognized at BCMS, with the coaching staff consisting of a well-trained group of dedicated individuals. The role of coaches is delineated in the following ways as described in the Barren County Middle School Athletic Policy: Middle school coaches

- Work under the guidelines established for the program by the BCMS principal, assistant principal, and athletic director.
- Work with other coaches to develop a coordinated program that builds skills and attitudes needed for success at the middle school level.
- Develop relationships with participants that are based on mutual respect and trust.
- Develop and maintain positive relationships with players, parents, officials, and other coaches.
- Understand that participation is a major goal in the program.
- Conduct themselves in a mature, responsible, and courteous manner.
- Deal with conflicts and disagreements in a polite and professional manner.
- Introduce and strengthen the skills needed for each participant to have the opportunity to experience success.
- Build and strengthen the confidence and self-esteem of all student athletes regardless of their abilities.
- Treat all participants with respect and as valued team members.
- Continue efforts to improve their own knowledge of the sport coached.
- Evaluate their success on how they have helped students become better players rather than on the win-loss record.

● ● ●

Barren County Middle School

Phone: 270.651.4909

http://www.barren.k12.ky.us/bcms/

Staffing intramural programs

As discussed previously, intramural sports programs do not exist in many middle schools and, where they exist, are often given low priority. This is a serious omission, for without intramural sports programs, a good many young adolescents will never have the opportunity to participate in sports as a part of their formal education.

Staffing intramural sports programs is a major consideration, and the decisions made regarding intramurals are just as important as those associated with interscholastic sports programs. These programs serve larger numbers of young adolescents and deserve strong support.

Unlike coaching assignments in interscholastic sports, where coaches are assigned to particular sports, directors of intramurals are typically responsible for all sports. Others, including volunteers, may be involved in directing and implementing the intramural sports program in large schools. Seventy-four percent of the schools in the authors' survey employ athletic directors; only 26 percent have intramural directors. This discrepancy is accounted for in part by the larger number of schools that have interscholastic sports but not intramural sports programs. However, this does not fully account for the wide discrepancy between the two staffing priorities. If intramurals sports programs are to play a significant role in providing sport opportunities for larger numbers of young adolescents, equitable staffing practices for them should exist as well.

Standards for intramural directors

Directors of middle level intramural sports programs have several roles. Here are some useful guidelines.

- *Effective intramural sports directors understand and support the high priority placed on intramural sports programs.* Intramurals should have a high priority and staffing based on the amount of time required for supervision and the number of participants. Too often staffing and funding are based more on the visibility and popularity of selected sports rather than the need for all young adolescents to take an active part. Intramural sports programs should not be viewed simply as an add-on to interscholastic sports programs or as an inexpensive means of providing sports participation to a large number of students. Although intramurals can be more cost efficient than interscholastic sports, they still need to be staffed and funded adequately to provide optimum opportunities for participants.

An increasing number of schools are reducing or eliminating interscholastic programs for financial reasons and moving to intramural programs. In such cases, schools should reallocate a portion of the money saved on transportation, uniforms, equipment, officials, and other expenses to strengthen intramural programs.

• *Effective middle level intramural sports directors are knowledgeable and dedicated to the success of their programs.* It is often difficult to find individuals who are willing and qualified to assume the responsibility for directing intramural programs. An intramural director position is usually a yearlong commitment and requires individuals to understand several sports and oversee several coaches or volunteers. Additionally, those who are most often qualified to direct an intramural program may also be the most qualified for and interested in coaching interscholastic sports. This is frequently the case in middle schools where both intramurals and interscholastic sports are offered. These individuals may be asked to coach, teach physical education or other subjects, and direct intramural programs at the same time. It is unrealistic and unfair to expect individuals to fulfill all of these responsibilities well. Every effort should be made to find individuals who are willing to direct the intramural programs and are not put in situations where multiple demands negatively affect the quality of the jobs they do when working with young adolescents. When individuals selected lack an understanding of young adolescent development and the middle school concept, that deficit should be taken care of by conversations, readings, and seminars.

• *Effective intramural directors use a team approach to run middle level intramural programs.* A team approach may be one solution to staffing middle level intramural sports programs. There are frequently middle level teachers who are capable and willing to be involved with intramural sports programs for part or all of the school year. Most middle schools are organized into academic teams that search for ways to extend the teaming approach into other aspects of the school. Securing a team to be responsible for the intramural program or a part of it has several advantages beyond solving a staffing problem. For those schools that offer both intramurals and interscholastic programs, a team approach can allow coaches to participate in intramural programs—instead of running the entire program—when they are not involved in coaching assignments. Team members could also assist in intramural sports for which they do not have primary responsibility. As with any effective middle school team, two things must be present to achieve success—adequate time to plan and a shared vision for the program.

- *Effective intramural directors understand and follow developmentally responsive philosophies.* Effective intramural programs have and adhere to a well-conceived philosophy that reflects the developmental realities of early adolescence. This philosophy should, of course, apply to the entire middle school sports program. Those directing the intramural program should be dedicated to seeing that this philosophy is carried out and visible to all involved in the program. One common belief that should be evident in the philosophy is the commitment to providing sports experiences for all students. A clear emphasis should be inclusive participation by as many young adolescents as possible regardless of their stage of physical development.

- *Effective intramural directors possess strong organizational skills.* In addition to a strong belief in what a middle school sports program should be, intramural directors must have effective organizational skills. Intramural programs are open to the entire student body; scheduling a wide variety of sports activities as well as other scheduling responsibilities—placing students on teams, providing proper supervision—demands a director with good organizational skills. In intramural programs, it is much easier to establish rules that reflect the needs and characteristics of young adolescents than with interscholastic sports. In addition, those individuals responsible for intramural programs should establish well-defined and effectively enforced rules for participation.

- *Effective intramural sports directors engage in continual program evaluation and use the results for program improvement.* For intramural programs to be successful, they must be evaluated on a regular basis and the information gained then used to enhance their quality. Surveys may be completed by students, teachers, and other stakeholders, and planned observations and comments of participants may be used to gather needed assessments. Evaluations should be formative and take place throughout the program so that adjustments can be made when needed during the school year.

Other responsibilities for directors of intramurals include (a) publicizing all rules and regulations; (b) determining which sports and related activities should be included in the program; (c) seeking adequate funding for the programs; and (d) devising recognition systems that focus more on successful teams rather than on individual performances.

In summary, developmentally responsive interscholastic and intramural sports programs must be staffed with qualified adults who have a commitment to making middle level sports programs a vital part of the total school program, embracing the developmental needs of every young adolescent enrolled.

Administrative support for middle level sports programs

Any successful educational program depends on the quality and commitment of the individuals directing the program, and a middle school sports program is certainly no exception. Critical, then, is the administrative support for sports programs. When the administrators do not consider intramural and interscholastic programs key components of a high-performing middle school, that view will be recognized and adopted by others. This is especially true for intramural sports programs, because they do not hold the entertainment value or bragging rights associated with interscholastics.

Principals and other administrators should understand, and help others understand, that effective sports programs can and should be a part of fully functioning middle level schools. The authors believe that these programs should be viewed as a part of the *curriculum* that schools offer all young adolescents, not extracurricular or even cocurricular. The argument here is not to claim that sports programs are as important as academic programs, but rather to affirm that, when developmentally responsive, these programs can and should be key parts of the overall learning opportunities provided for young adolescents.

One of the primary responsibilities of middle level principals is to help establish and maintain a developmentally appropriate vision for their school. This can be challenging when it comes to sports programs, as middle level principals are inevitably confronted with internal and outside pressures regarding the nature and priorities given to interscholastic versus intramural sports programs. Typically principals are pressured to give the majority of all resources, including human resources, to interscholastic team sports while providing only limited support for intramural programs.

Principals must also deal effectively with parents, members of the community, rival schools, and educators who are interested only in competitive sports with little or no interest in also having successful intramural sports for young adolescents. These administrators must also deal with high school coaches who may view the middle level as a training ground for high school sports programs. In many communities there are also club sports programs as well as other non-school-sponsored sports programs that affect middle school sports programs in multiple ways.

In Summary

It bears repeating—the most critical element in successful, developmentally responsive middle level intramural and interscholastic sports programs is qualified and committed coaches. Coaches are on the frontlines working with parents, other educators, and the general public; their responsibilities are many and varied. And, of course, their daily interactions with middle level students are often the deciding factor whether the sport experience is a good one or one never to be repeated.

In this chapter we have discussed the issues surrounding new teachers who also coach and the challenges of part-time coaches who are not part of the school where they coach. The key, of course, for all coaches at the middle school level is that they know young adolescents. Respondents to our survey indicated time and time again that knowledge of this 10- to 15-year-old age group is even more important than knowing the sport.

We ended with a useful list of effective practices, information on staffing intramural programs, and standards for intramural directors. The challenges discussed in this chapter must be faced with diligence and courage by all who are responsible for the education and well-being of young adolescents. ●

6.
PARENTS AND MIDDLE SCHOOL SPORTS

Who Is This Game For?

At age 13, Danielle is in her ninth season of playing organized soccer. She is an excellent player for her age as attested by the dozens of trophies and ribbons overflowing from her bedroom into the living room. Turn the corner into the kitchen and another symbol of the prominence of Danielle's soccer career stares you in the face—a 3' x 5' bulletin board listing every practice, game, summer camp, and meeting for the three different teams she plays on every year. While Danielle plays for her eighth-grade team at Madison Middle School, that is a minor part of her schedule. Her mother often picks her up before the end of a practice to rush her to travel team practice. She travels to tournaments nearly every weekend year-round. She often wishes she could play basketball or volleyball with her classmates, but she gave up those activites long ago. Make no mistake: This is not a leisure time pursuit. For Danielle's family, soccer is their life; parents' work schedules and family time is scheduled around soccer games and tournaments. The goal—a full college scholarship for Danielle. Lately, Danielle wonders if she wants soccer to be such a large part of her life. Sometimes she would just like to be a normal 13-year-old.

Parents are frequently surprised when their young adolescent sons and daughters announce that there is no need for them to attend their sporting events. Since most parents have always attended their children's games, they may not realize that their children appreciate the support when their parents attend—but are concerned that they will embarrass them in front of their friends. At such times, it is important to remember that peer pressure is a naturally occurring developmental characteristic and a powerful determiner of behavior during early adolescence. As with many issues that arise as children leave childhood, parents' roles are also dramatically changed. Parents will play very different roles in their young adolescent's sports career during the middle school years.

Whether leading to positive or negative overall effects, youth sports have become major spectator sports in many towns and cities. Games and other competitions do not draw thousands of fans to any one playing field at one time and are not broadcast to millions of viewers across the nation, but parents and other spectators gather by the hundreds in parks and stadiums to watch youth sports competitions every week. If all of these spectators were lumped together, many stadiums across the country would be filled.

The increasing popularity of youth sports has had a dramatic effect on school sports programs, particularly at the middle level. In the past, the majority of youngsters were first introduced to organized competitive sports when they reached middle school. Now children participate in organized sports as young as preschool, and by the time they reach middle school they have certain expectations—as do their parents—about playing time, the importance of winning and losing, and many other issues.

The changing roles of parents

Informal sports are typically those that are organized by participants themselves, while formal sports are those with established rules organized by adults (Coakley, 1987; 2004). Youth sports have moved away from informal sports and toward formal sports over recent decades. This move toward early involvement of children and young adolescents in formal, organized sports competitions has also resulted in major changes in the roles of parents and other family members in relation to sports activities. One obvious result is that family members have become involved in the sports activities of their children at younger and younger ages. When children were primarily involved in informal sports

Youth sports have moved away from informal sports and toward formal sports over recent decades.

in neighborhoods—the old sandlot—the role of parents was minimal. With the increasing involvement of children in formal sports, parents have become much more engaged in getting their children to practice, attending their games, and buying equipment. They often become designated drivers, scorekeepers, timers, seekers of sponsors, and takers of other tasks (Murphy, 1999).

As their children reach middle school, some parents have difficulty when these roles are taken over by others in school-sponsored sports programs. Some who resist the changes need help in understanding how to back away and learn ways to provide support at the middle level. This renewed understanding of proper roles for middle school parents in school-sponsored sports requires effort on the part of school officials and can lead to positive relationships among parents, young adolescent athletes, coaches, and the community.

Making this transition from youth sports to middle school sports is easier for some parents than for others. Some are able to function in the dual roles of youth sports parent and middle school parent with much success. Parents may have a younger son or daughter who still participates in youth sports, or a middle school child who participates in both club sports and middle school sports. This can be a positive situation if parents can distinguish between the two roles, or a negative one if they confuse them. The message to parents and other family members should not be that their involvement in school-sponsored sports is no longer wanted or valued, but rather that the nature of their involvement needs to be different. Carefully planned educational meetings should be provided for all parents regarding ways they can be involved in supporting both their children and developmentally responsive sports programs.

A second discrepancy also exists, and may be even more difficult for some parents—different expectations for middle school sports and high school sports. Some parents believe that the primary purpose of middle school sports should be to prepare their children to perform well in high school and thus see their roles as similar to that of high school parents. Parents who expect middle school sports to be equivalent to high school sports have unrealistic expectations for training and competition. These are more often appropriate for high school athletes, but definitely not for young adolescent athletes. In some cases, parents are already envisioning a college athletic scholarship for their children, but only if the middle school provides a highly competitive focus. It is critical that those responsible for middle level sports programs work hard to help parents and other influential adults better understand the roles they should play in developmentally responsive sports programs.

Educating parents about middle school sports

Middle school parent meetings before each sports season or at the beginning of intramural programs are excellent vehicles for educating and involving parents. A general meeting for all parents about sports programs should help them gain a better understanding of the unique purpose of middle school sports and how they can be supportive. Such meetings should always begin by focusing on the sports philosophy of the school. Unfortunately, these well-intentioned meetings often fall short of their intended purpose because the school sports philosophy and its implications for parents and other family members are not fully explained and no dialogue with parents takes place. These meetings tend to focus too intently on schedules, past successes, predictions for upcoming seasons, and booster clubs rather than on the basic purposes of intramural and interscholastic sports programs. The prime purpose of these meetings is to help parents understand the nature and practices of developmentally responsive sports programs as well as their roles in these programs.

After a presentation and discussion of the middle school philosophy as it relates to the sports program, the meeting can be broken down by sports, including intramural programs, allowing parents to rotate to the various coaches for a more detailed description of each program. In small schools where one person coaches more than one sport, it may be more appropriate to give an overview of the school's sports philosophy and have coaches give brief descriptions of each sport. Coaches for each sport can then have a follow-up meeting for parents before each sports season begins. These individual meetings will provide parents with more specific information and offer another opportunity to reemphasize the sports program's philosophy.

A similar format might also be used for students who are currently participating, or planning to participate, in middle school sports programs. Meetings at the beginning of the school year can familiarize students with the purposes of sports programs and provide opportunities to learn more about how to become involved.

Middle school sports philosophy

The purposes and philosophy of middle school sports programs should be clearly stated in some form for other school personnel, officials, and members of the community. If the school is in a league or conference, it is appropriate to send a copy of this information to other schools in the conference.

There is no single, universal sports philosophy that should guide and direct all middle school sports programs. Just as middle schools are uniquely different from elementary or high schools, each middle school has its own unique identity. Thus a sports philosophy should be developed by the school with input from all stakeholders.

In the authors' sports survey, 86 percent of the middle schools surveyed reported that they had already developed a philosophy for their sports program. Although these schools should be applauded for what they have developed, the real challenge is to examine that philosophy in light of what they are actually practicing and look for ways to more fully implement that philosophy. For many schools, a reexamination may point out that the stated philosophy is not fully in line with the middle school concept.

Parents' views of middle school sports

Although it is essential for parents to have an understanding of the purpose and philosophy of a middle school sports program, making them aware of their roles and responsibilities is equally critical. Contrary to what some people believe, most parents and schools want the same thing—effective sports programs that serve their children well. In one study where parents were surveyed about the characteristics they expected in a coach, the following were identified—listed here in order of their importance (Schenkenfelder, 2000):

1. Demonstrates knowledge about the sport coached
2. Exhibits sportsmanship
3. Communicates effectively
4. Serves as a good role model
5. Demonstrates patience
6. Encourages players
7. Provides individual instruction
8. Provides equal playing time for participants
9. Produces winning teams. (pp. 49-50)

All of these are attributes that should be reflected in middle school sports program philosophies. In fact, a survey of student athletes discovered that they too favor a sports program that is developmentally responsive to their needs. When asked how they viewed the importance of their various athletic experiences, they responded in the following ways (Schenkenfelder, 2000, p. 29):

Experience	Response
Playing every game	82% very important
Attending every practice	90% very important
Having fun at practice and games	83% very important
Demonstrating good sportsmanship	85% very important

Building the foundation for a middle school sports program that can and will be supported by parents is sometimes difficult; the greater challenge may be effectively communicating to parents and other stakeholders their roles in implementing that philosophy on a daily basis. This is especially true if middle school sports programs have established histories of programs and practices that are not based on what is known about the needs and characteristics of young adolescents. As most people readily recognize, it is frequently difficult to break long-standing traditions that reflect the desires of adults rather than those of students.

Core practices for parents

An excellent listing of parents' roles or expectations is the following set of core practices for parents of student athletes (University of Maine, 2005):

- Parents give consistent encouragement and support to their children regardless of the degree of success, the level of skill, or time on the field.
- Parents stress the importance of respect for coaches through discussion with their children, and highlight the critical nature of the coaches' contributions to the team and its success.
- Parents attend school meetings at the outset of sports seasons to meet coaches and school officials and learn firsthand about the expectation of participation in interscholastic athletics.
- Parents serve as role models, see the "big picture," and support all programs and athletes.
- Parents agree to abide by the school rules guiding the conduct of sports, modeling the principles for their student athletes.
- Parents ensure a balance in student athletes' lives, encouraging participation in multiple sports and activities with academics placed first and foremost.
- Parents leave coaching to coaches and do not criticize coaching strategies or team performance. They avoid putting pressure on their children about playing time and performance. (p. 8)

Although this list of suggestions is excellent, it remains for middle schools to assist students, parents, school personnel, and others in carrying out these practices in their individual schools. Many or all of these core practices may reflect the roles schools expect parents to play, but if sports practices at school do not match stated philosophies, mixed messages will be sent and received by parents and others. These core principles can serve as guides in helping establish clearly stated roles for parents that will enable them to be supportive of their children's participation in middle school sports programs built on a sound philosophical base.

Parents as sports fans

Encouraging parents to be a part of their children's sports activities is a program goal. But there are occasions when the participation of parents is inappropriate and damaging to the program's goals. Negative behaviors on the part of parents and other spectators may be spontaneous and unintentional when they get caught up in the excitement of the game and their emotions overtake common sense, but this does not excuse nor negate the damage that can come from such behaviors. Holding discussions with parents about proper behavior while attending athletic events is in order.

The authors of *Just Let The Kids Play* (Bigelow, Moroney, & Hall, 2001) cite several examples of parents' losing control at sporting events. One case involved 50 to 60 parents of middle school age football players who engaged in a furious fistfight after a football game. The adults kicked, punched, and screamed at each other in a ten-minute melee caught on videotape and shown on the local news. In another case cited by Schenkenfelder (2000), a grandmother was arrested when she assaulted an official during halftime of one of her granddaughters' basketball games. The referee happened to be an off-duty police officer, and when she was physically attacked, she went to her police car where she retrieved a pair of handcuffs and called for backup. She then proceeded to go back into the gym and arrest the grandmother. Although these incidents rarely happen at middle level sporting events, they are happening with more frequency in youth sports as well as in high school sports. Middle school sports programs are not immune to such misbehaviors, and those responsible should be proactive in preventing them.

One of the keys to teaching and coaching at the middle level is the ability to channel the energies of young adolescents in productive and positive directions. The same skills might also be applied to middle school parents. Votano (2000) presents a list of "Ten Things Parents Don't Get About Kids and Sports."

1. Don't tell your kids how to do this or that during car rides to games or practices.
2. Kids can get psyched for a game without parents' help.
3. It is the duty of parents to sit quietly and watch their kids do wonderful things, not, however, when they miss a game or yak it up with their friends in the stands.
4. If parents don't know what they're talking about, kids don't want them to talk.
5. Even if a parent knows what they are talking about, kids don't want them to talk (unless they are the coach).
6. Kids wish parents would practice what they preach about sportsmanship and not blame the officials or argue with them.
7. Kids often can't hear parents yelling when they're concentrating on playing, but sometimes they can; and either way they don't like it.
8. After a loss, kids don't want to be told it doesn't matter.
9. Also after a loss, kids don't want to be told it does matter.
10. Kids say they just want to have fun, and parents don't get it. Besides, they would rather play on a losing team than sit on the bench on a winning one. Also they say their parents take it too seriously—"they act like it is school" (p. 38).

Although these may be unwanted parent behaviors, there are more serious behaviors involving children and their parents that have more lasting impacts on athletes and school sports programs.

Soccer is becoming an increasingly popular sport for middle school students.

Freeport Middle School—Parents as Partners in Sports

Freeport Middle School

Phone: 207.865.6051

http://fms.freeportpublicschools.org/

Freeport Middle School (ME) has an enrollment of approximately 325 in grades six, seven, and eight. FMS exists to serve the unique academic, physical, social, and emotional needs of young adolescents. The staff of Freeport Middle School is committed to creating and maintaining an orderly, trusting, and caring environment where teaching and learning are exciting and students are assisted as they develop responsibility. All aspects of the school's organization, curricular and cocurricular activities, are child centered and designed to accommodate individual learning styles so that all may experience success.

Educators at FMS understand that parent involvement during the middle school years is crucial in determining school effectiveness. The information below, prepared by the Freeport Athletics Office, is used at FMS. This information is representative of ways middle schools can encourage parents and other family members to create positive learning environments for middle school sports programs.

Parent roles and responsibilities
Parents should
- Remain in spectator areas during contests.
- Not make derogatory comments directed towards officials, coaches, or players on either team.
- Not officiate from the sidelines.
- Control emotions.
- Show interest, enthusiasm, and support for their children.
- Demonstrate and promote positive values and characteristics of good sportsmanship.
- Not question or criticize coaches' decisions in front of their children.
- Realize that athletics is an integral part of the school's total curriculum and that coaches are there to help facilitate learning.

What to say to your child during pre-game and post-game conversations
- Pre-game: I love you. What do you want for dinner? and Good luck!
- Post-game: Nice game! What do you want for dinner? and I love you.

What parents should expect from coaches
- The philosophy of the coaches and programs should be communicated.
- Individual and team expectations should be made clear.
- Location and times of all practices and contests should be shared.
- All team requirements should be available.
- Procedures followed in case of injury should be provided.
- Discipline actions that may result in the denial of child's participation should be delineated.

What coaches should expect from parents
- Concerns should be expressed directly to the coach.
- Notification of schedule conflicts should be made well in advance.
- Specific concerns with regard to a coach's philosophy and expectations should be communicated.

- Support for the attributes of dedication, commitment, and responsibility should be expressed and demonstrated.
- All student athletes should be encouraged to excel.

What concerns to discuss with coaches
- Concern about the treatment of your child, mentally or physically, should be expressed.
- Ways to help student athletes develop and improve are valid topics for discussion and collaboration.
- Concerns about your child's behavior should be expressed.

What issues not to discuss with coaches
- The playing time for your child.
- Team strategies.
- Play calling.
- Other student athletes and their performance.

● ● ●

Damaging parent behaviors

One of the most damaging behaviors occurs when parents hold unrealistic performance expectations for their sons or daughters. This puts undue pressure on the other athletes and the coaches. With parents becoming involved in their children's sports activities at earlier ages, initial expectations are often unrealistic. For example, early maturing youth may lose their advantage as their peers become more physically mature and therefore more competitive. Additionally, it is common for more individuals to be trying out for fewer slots on teams as children move from elementary schools to middle schools and from middle schools to high schools. These athletes may begin to lose their edge of early maturity and athletic success and need parents and other significant adults to understand and accept their levels of performance.

Excessive pressure by parents on their children to achieve can be the result of what is called *achievement through proxy syndrome* (Bigelow, Moroney, & Hall, 2001, p. 80). This is usually a "dad thing" but is also increasingly becoming a "mom thing." It occurs when parents are trying to relive their sports careers, or live fantasy sports careers, through their children. These parents gauge their children's sports success according to how they developed, or wished they had developed, and set expectations that equal or exceed what they themselves achieved. By using their own sports ambitions as a measuring stick for their children, their children are often placed in a sport that the parent selects rather than one they enjoy or in which they have the best chance of being successful.

Middle school should be a time to participate widely in a number of sports—not a time to specialize in only one. This certainly does not mean that middle school athletes should not participate in the sport for which they have talent, but this may be the last opportunity they have to participate in any other sport. They may even discover that they have talent in multiple sports. One of the dangers in single sports specialization is the likelihood of overuse injuries. These can be very damaging and even end young adolescents' sports participation before they have time to mature and develop their skills to pursue the sport at the high school level. Another common result of too early specialization is attrition or burnout.

> *Middle school should be a time to participate widely in a number of sports—not a time to specialize in only one.*

In Summary

Parents, school personnel, and others should think of young adolescents' participation in athletics as a journey, not a destination. Frequently, parents focus too intently on how middle school sports can make their children more successful in high school and college athletics. It is important for parents to enjoy and support their children's participation in middle school sports for what it is at that time in their lives, not for what it might do for their future success in sports. This does not mean that setting future goals is not important or that talented athletic performers should not be encouraged to improve their skills and abilities. However, the primary focus of all middle level sports programs should be on more immediate goals such as mastering basic skills, conditioning, and improving performance.

At the middle school level, young adolescents should select the sports in which they wish to participate and then should participate in the safest and most joyful ways possible. Parents should be involved in decisions about sports participation, but the final decisions should be left to young adolescents.

Positive parental involvement is critical to any effective middle school. Sports are a prime avenue for parents to be a part of their children's school activities. Middle schools should capitalize on this opportunity to involve parents and help them understand and appreciate the roles they can play in maximizing their children's sports experiences. ●

7.
RECOMMENDATIONS FOR MIDDLE LEVEL SPORTS

Like the call for a higher academic literacy for all our students, there is a clear need to make a series of mid-course corrections in our efforts to offer student athletes healthy learning experiences through sports.

—*Sports Done Right*

The authors hope that focusing attention on issues and concerns related to middle school sports will raise the awareness level of all stakeholders and lead to actions that will make middle school sports more developmentally responsive. Only when problems are recognized and new possibilities explored can actions be taken to ensure all young adolescents have opportunities to participate in intramural and interscholastic programs that serve them well. In many cases this means breaking away from some practices that are traditional and satisfactory in the view of many adults. The authors are well aware of the benefits that occur when young adolescents participate in interscholastic sports and do not want to curtail them. Rather, the central thesis of this book is that interscholastic sports as well as intramurals should be developmentally responsive—based on the needs and characteristics of young adolescents—in order to be most effective for all students.

The recommendations that follow are not all-encompassing but will provide beginning points for actions as new middle level sports programs are created and existing ones are evaluated for potential improvements.

Developmentally responsive middle level sports programs

Middle level literature, research, and successful practice make it clear that effective middle schools meet not only the academic needs of young adolescents but also their physical, social, and emotional needs. It is also evident that these realms of developmental characteristics are so interdependent that one cannot be addressed without affecting the others. This has been well documented in effective middle school classrooms, where conscientious efforts to adapt curriculum and instruction to address the developmental needs of their students have been successful (NMSA, 2003).

If effective middle schools are based on meeting the developmental needs of young adolescents, the same approach should apply to intramural and interscholastic sports programs. Unfortunately, many middle level sports programs continue to mimic those at the senior high school level. Even in middle schools that are developmentally responsive in other aspects of schooling, it is all too typical for sports programs to remain relatively unchanged from those of junior and senior high schools. It seems that middle level sports, especially interscholastic sports, have been immune to reform as other middle level programs and practices have undergone scrutiny and improvement. As a result, the majority of middle level sports programs seem to be designed for older adolescents or adults instead of based on the developmental realities of early adolescence. This situation ignores and denies what we know as these youngsters experience what is perhaps the most formative stage of their lives.

It is very important to understand that middle school sports issues are not determined by a school's name or grade configuration, but rather about what is best for students in this developmental stage wherever they are enrolled. While we have used the terms middle school and middle level throughout the book to refer to all schools for young adolescents, the many different grade configurations in different parts of the country, including K-8, 7-12, and K-12, obviously include young adolescents. These principles and recommendations apply equally to them. In effective middle level schools, all intramural and interscholastic sports programs, as well as other cocurricular activities, should adhere to the same philosophy that guides other aspects of successful schooling. To do less is to compromise the school's commitment to providing an education that is appropriate for young adolescents. This challenging task calls for courageous, collaborative leadership on the part of the administrators, athletic directors, coaches, and others who support or are interested in middle school sports.

Many middle schools have implemented developmentally responsive sports programs, and much can be learned from the successes of these schools. Examples of such programs have been provided throughout this book. For these schools it will be a matter of maintaining and refining what they already have established. For a great many other schools, however, the task will be more challenging. But it must be faced if middle level schools and their programs are to be truly committed to creating effective educational environments for young adolescents. The often touted advantages of young adolescents' participating in sports can be realized, but only if schools look carefully at their sports programs and make them consistent with the shared vision that encompasses *all* aspects of any middle level school. Everyone responsible must work continually to see that vision implemented.

This book focuses attention on middle school sports, an area that has received little attention over the last two decades, and it discusses the implications of applying the middle school concept to sports programs. To those ends, the authors have (a) documented the status of sports programs in American middle schools via a national survey; (b) reviewed the literature and research on middle school sports; and (c) examined selected issues facing middle school sports programs. The following recommendations provide a framework for individual schools and districts to consider in assessing all aspects of their intramural and interscholastic sports programs. These recommendations should stimulate discussions that will lead to actions in improving middle level sports programs.

Recommendation 1: Develop a clearly stated, developmentally responsive sports philosophy for all middle level sports programs, one that is widely understood and used by all stakeholders.
The more the general philosophy of the school is understood by administrators, teachers, students, parents, community members, and others, the more it becomes a reality in the daily functions of the school, including the sports program.

Schools without a written sports philosophy run the risk of having programs that are haphazardly organized and characterized by inconsistent and inequitable practices. Clearly stated philosophies give coaches and others involved needed direction for making the many decisions they face daily

Clearly stated philosophies give coaches and others involved needed direction for making the many decisions they face daily.

as they work to provide young adolescents with quality sports opportunities. Well-articulated sports philosophies also provide administrators with the support they need when dealing with contentious issues that inevitably arise from parents, community members, and others who may have differing views about middle school sports.

Simply having a well-written sports philosophy is of little value, of course, if the philosophy espoused is not reflected in the daily operations of the sports programs. If providing all middle level students with opportunities to participate is a part of a school's sports philosophy, this belief should underlie coaches' strategies about playing time and be clearly understood by students and parents. Copies of sports programs' philosophies should be made available to all parents, not just those whose children are currently participating in sports. Meetings for all parents should be held at the beginning of the year to inform them of the beliefs that underlie the specific regulations and procedures. Also, at the beginning of each sports season, coaches should review with all athletes the school's sports philosophy.

Middle schools that already have a sports philosophy should review it regularly to ensure that programs are authentically developmentally responsive and that the philosophy is widely understood and clearly evident in the actual practices of intramural and interscholastic sports programs. No matter whether the philosophy is being reexamined or being developed, the underpinning question that must guide its formation should be: *Does the philosophy point toward a developmentally appropriate sports program?* The sports program philosophy should become a living document, shared and supported by all who are involved in the school sports program.

Recommendation 2: Offer a sports program that includes intramurals and interscholastics, both with a high priority. Sports programs should provide opportunities for all young adolescents to participate in some sports activities regardless of their stage of physical development, size, exceptionality, gender, or any of the other differences that characterize 10- to 15-year-olds. Middle level sports programs should provide a balance between intramural and interscholastic sports programs so that all young adolescents can reap the potential benefits of participation. Unfortunately, many middle schools offer only interscholastic sports, with limited or no support for high quality intramural sports. For example, the authors' national survey found that only 58 percent of middle schools had intramural programs, while 96 percent had interscholastic programs. Not only is the percentage of middle schools with intramural sports programs relatively small, but the percentage has been declining for many years (McEwin, Dickinson, & Jenkins, 2003). This is a trend that needs to be reversed.

Providing the needed balance between intramural and interscholastic sports is a real challenge, one that has to be addressed successfully if sports programs are to serve all young adolescents equitably and well. The good news is that middle schools with balanced sports programs do exist and can serve as models for other schools. In these schools, all young adolescents, including those who play on school teams, have opportunities for participating in intramural sports activities. If young adolescents are given the opportunity to explore, participate, develop skills, and build positive attitudes toward sports participation, both intramural and interscholastic sports programs must be inclusive and rewarding for participants. Eighty-three percent of respondents to the survey supported such comprehensive sports programs.

Although it is a challenge to develop and maintain developmentally responsive middle level sports programs, it is crucial that this goal be accomplished. Incorporating the recommendations in this chapter into an interscholastic program will require a firm commitment on the part of administrators, coaches, and other stakeholders; inevitably, opposition will be encountered. Substantive efforts and courageous leadership will be required for success. The end result, however, will be worth the effort, for a developmentally responsive interscholastic sports program will be an accomplishment of significance, especially for the student athletes it serves.

It would seem that implementing a comprehensive, developmentally responsive intramural program would be more easily accomplished than developing and maintaining such an interscholastic program. However, intramural programs have typically had a very low priority in most middle schools, so many of the existing programs are marginal in value. This frequently means that new funds must be found to reform these programs. An additional problem will be to gain support from parents and community members who have traditionally viewed interscholastic sports as *the* only level of sports; it may be especially difficult to gain the support of parents who see the role of middle level sports as preparing young adolescents to participate in high school sports. No matter what the level of difficulty, however, intramural programs need to be established and maintained so that large numbers of young adolescents can benefit from participating in a wide variety of individual and team sports. As is the case with interscholastic sports programs, the recommendations in this chapter should be used to guide the establishment and refinement of intramural programs.

Recommendation 3: Operate intramural and interscholastic sports programs that maximize the enjoyment of participants. This means, among other things, that these programs should not be so competitive that participants experience undue stress. As noted in Chapter 3, when stress levels become very high and only a select few dominate the playing time, many young adolescents drop out of sports altogether. When interscholastic sports are organized in ways that are overly competitive, the resulting pressures can become counterproductive to the purposes of successful middle school sports programs. The emphasis in middle school sports programs should be placed on enhancing self-esteem and developing social and physical skills within reasonably competitive environments.

All young adolescents who participate in interscholastic or intramural sports want to win. However, when winning becomes more important than the enjoyment of participating, students often become disenchanted. This does not mean that sports experiences for young adolescents will never include disappointments. There will be times when their individual performances are not as good as they expected or times when their teams lose, but this is a part of sports competition. When sports environments are healthy, these disappointments are typically short-lived and middle level athletes continue to enjoy and benefit from their sports participation.

Practices used in interscholastic sports programs can discourage young athletes from participating in a sport. Coaches who over-stress conditioning at the expense of having fun run the risk of having middle level students become bored and lose interest in participating. Middle school sports should turn budding athletes on to sports rather than discourage them from further participation. The degree to which young adolescents enjoy practices is a key factor in determining whether they drop out or remain in sports during the middle school years. At this very formative time in their development, middle level students should be encouraged to enjoy their sports participation and not be subjected to the effects of intense pressure from parents and coaches. Practices should offer opportunities for young adolescents to gain confidence in their abilities while discovering their interests and talents. In the long run, this will lead to their becoming better athletes.

Recommendation 4: Organize and administer middle school sports programs in ways that encourage young adolescents to explore multiple sports rather than specialize in one sport to the exclusion of others. Young adolescents are changing in every aspect of their lives. At no other time in their lives will they experience so many physical, cognitive, social, and emotional changes. These young people are discovering who they are and beginning to understand the roles they will play as they become more mature. This stage is the ideal one for young adolescents to explore different sports and select the ones where they receive the most pleasure and experience the most success. As they grow and mature physically, they may discover that they have talents and interests in a variety of sports. As athletic abilities begin to emerge, young adolescents will have ample opportunity to pursue one or more sports in high school. As previously noted, early and intense specialization in one sport also leads to overuse injuries and contributes to middle level athletes' becoming burned out on sports participation.

Intramurals should provide young adolescents with many opportunities to experience several different competitive sports as well as lifetime sports. On the other hand, interscholastic sports are more limited in number and typically involve a small percentage of the school's population. Additionally, overlapping seasons frequently require individuals to select one sport for participation during a given time period. Therefore, middle level sports programs need to be carefully planned in ways that permit and encourage young adolescents to explore several sports.

Participating in a variety of sports has many advantages. For example, it provides excellent opportunities for young adolescents to associate with different peers as teammates. For many young adolescents, being a part of a team is just as meaningful as excelling in a sport. Too often when students specialize exclusively in a sport at a young age, non-inclusive cliques develop which can be very damaging to the well-being of all concerned.

Unfortunately, the trend in youth sports is toward specialization rather than exploration. As previously noted, children in youth sports often specialize in one sport, playing it year-round and joining club travel teams. By the time these young adolescents reach the middle level, they have already committed to a given sport. This trend should be considered when those responsible for middle level sports programs are seeking ways to ensure that multiple sports experiences are provided for all students. Intramural sports programs should be inclusive of all middle school students.

It is important that parents and other key individuals understand that one thing all young adolescents have in common is that they are still developing. It is rare for 10- to 15-year-olds to reach their peak performance in a sport. Although a few Olympic gymnasts have come close to reaching that peak at such early ages, they are the exceptions rather than the rule. Middle level sports programs should accommodate all students regardless of their stage of development or degree of success on the playing fields.

Recommendation 5: Establish clearly articulated and equitable eligibility polices that support the school's commitment to academics. Although sports play an important part of a middle school's educational environment, academics must always be the number one priority for all young adolescent students. Establishing a working relationship between sports and academics can be problematic. While teachers and coaches want students to be successful in classrooms as well as on the athletic fields, the academic performance of individuals frequently becomes a problem requiring carefully planned and widely understood eligibility policies.

An important missing link in many eligibility policies is a mechanism to assist students in becoming eligible again once they have been declared ineligible. Too often students declared ineligible are left to their own resources to regain eligibility. This frequently leads to failure both in the classroom and on the athletic field. Eligibility policies should outline the procedures that can be used by students to regain their eligibility. Steps taken to assist such students may be as simple as presenting them with a list of clearly stated options, such as (a) setting up times to visit with the teachers of classes in which they are having difficulty; (b) attending study hall during practice times; (c) spending time with their advisors for assistance; (d) participating in tutoring sessions before, during, or after school; and (e) having conferences with parents, teachers, and coaches. Eligibility policies should set up clear lines of communication between teachers and coaches. Teachers need to inform coaches in a timely manner if student athletes are falling behind in their academic progress instead of waiting until it is too late to remedy the situation. This is especially important in situations where playing seasons are short. If students cannot make up the work in three to four weeks, they are likely to miss the entire season. Likewise, coaches need to demonstrate initiative in working closely with teachers of students who are likely to have academic difficulties.

Eligibility policies should also deal directly with conduct issues. The recommendations suggested above dealing with academic eligibility should also apply to eligibility related to student conduct. Depending on the severity of the conduct, students should have the same kinds of options to become eligible again. However, these cases may involve coaches, administrators, advisors, parents, and other school and community professional personnel. Simply put, academic success for all young adolescents should be of utmost importance when designing and implementing eligibility policies that promote student learning and ethical behavior.

Recommendation 6: Employ middle level coaches who are knowledgeable about the nature of developmentally responsive middle school sports programs and committed to implementing them. This We Believe: Successful Schools for Young Adolescents (NMSA, 2003) states that "Successful schools for young adolescents are characterized by a culture that includes educators who value working with young adolescents and are prepared to do so" (p. 9). This applies to coaches as well as other middle level professionals. Just as teachers should be very knowledgeable about the subjects they teach, coaches should be knowledgeable about the sports they coach and the implications of those sports for the well-being of middle level students. Effective coaching helps athletes acquire the skills, attitudes, and conditioning to be successful. This requires more than knowledge of a particular sport. It calls for the ability to motivate and inspire athletes to reach their potential. The only way this can be effectively done is by understanding what motivates young adolescents. For coaches this means they must understand the developmental changes that are occurring in students' lives. This is more than just understanding the physical growth and development; it includes the interrelated cognitive, social, and emotional changes.

Although there are effective middle school coaches who do not teach, it is much more likely that coaches who are middle level teachers working daily with young adolescents will better understand them and the implications of their development for sports participation. Therefore, middle level educators with an interest and background in coaching should be the first priority when hiring coaches. When outside coaches are used, great care should be taken to make sure they understand the age group. Coaches not as familiar with this age group should be closely supervised, offered opportunities to work with more experienced middle level coaches, and participate in relevant professional development activities.

The pressure to win, experienced by high school coaches and athletes, should be minimized at the middle level. Middle school coaches should not feel forced to sacrifice teaching skills to all team members or to take other steps that reduce the enjoyment of participation because of an overemphasis on winning. Coaches as well as young adolescent athletes should be free to experience the joys that occur from just participating. Sports provide excellent opportunities for coaches and athletes to build positive, mutually beneficial relationships. Young adolescents need good adult role models, and who better than coaches to be significant others in their lives? Highly successful middle level coaches care about the overall welfare of all their players, helping them reach their full potential.

Recommendation 7: Assign a top priority to making middle school sports programs as safe as possible. As documented in Chapter 3, the most dangerous period to participate in competitive sports is early adolescence. Students aged 10 to 15 are especially susceptible to injury due to the softness of their growing bones and the relative tightness of their ligaments, tendons, and muscles. Steps to make sports participation safer and more rewarding for young adolescents include (a) step up adult supervision of all middle level sports activities; (b) establish clear and high standards for hiring and retaining middle level coaches; (c) mount community-wide campaigns to educate parents and communities about safe and developmentally responsive sports programs; (d) ensure that safe equipment is used and that playing fields and other facilities are safe and well-maintained; (e) require that all participants undergo full physical examinations before a season begins; (f) make careful, data-based decisions about which sports to include in an interscholastic sports program; (g) modify rules for playing sports in ways that reduce injuries; and (h) implement high quality intramural sports programs that are inclusive and designed for wide, safe participation (McEwin & Dickinson, 1997).

One of the greatest dangers for young adolescents participating in sports programs is that adults responsible for those programs are not aware of the dangers present or simply ignore the dangers inherent in middle level sports participation. It is essential that all those responsible for middle level sports take the necessary steps to ensure that participation does not result in serious injuries, disabilities, or even death. Coaches, administrators, parents, and other stakeholders must work together to make middle level sports as safe as possible for all participants. Initiatives to make this happen require courage and tenacity.

Recommendation 8: Make extensive efforts to help parents understand productive and appropriate ways they can be involved in supporting their children in middle level interscholastic and intramural sports programs. Most parents want to be involved, at least to some extent, in their children's school activities. Middle school sports can provide ideal opportunities for parents to become involved in positive and supportive ways. However, the roles parents and other family members play typically change during the middle school years, and they need help in understanding the changes and their new roles.

Once parents are educated about the school's philosophy and how to provide positive support for their children, they will support developmentally responsive sports programs that provide opportunities for more young adolescents and make safety a priority. Orientation meetings, well-designed brochures describing the sports program and its philosophy, and information posted on the school Web site are excellent methods to keep parents informed. Any information provided should focus on both intramural and interscholastic sports programs and include eligibility policies, behavior expectations, and expectations of coaches. It is also critical that parents be aware of expectations for them as both supportive parents and fans at sporting events. Some middle schools have improved parent behavior at sporting events by requiring parents to sign agreements that they and their children will abide by.

Parents and other stakeholders should always remember that middle level students are at a pivotal point in their development, when they are likely to make important decisions regarding their current and future involvement in sports activities. This is a time when young adolescents can be turned on or turned off to sports participation. Given opportunities to participate in developmentally responsive sports programs, they can learn many important lessons for life, including what it means to win and lose. It is a time when they need support and encouragement from their coaches, teammates, and most of all, their parents and other family members.

Recommendation 9: Establish rules governing middle school sports that will ensure the widest possible degree of participation by all team members. Many, if not all of the rules and regulations that govern middle school sports have been handed down from senior high schools. As has been previously pointed out, these rules and regulations designed for older adolescents and adults are not sufficient or appropriate for 10- to 15-year-olds.

In addition to establishing rules that are more developmentally responsive for young adolescents, modified rules can also provide opportunities for larger numbers of students to participate. As with other recommendations included in this chapter, it will likely require courage and much persistence to convince some people that a sport can be played by more than one set of rules. It is this break with tradition that makes many people uncomfortable.

Recommendation 10: Provide adequate and equitably balanced human and financial resources for all phases of middle level sports activities. For both interscholastic and intramural sports programs to have a high priority in middle schools, it is essential that both programs receive the support needed to be successful. Traditionally, disproportionate amounts of resources have been provided for interscholastic sports programs, which often serve fewer students, with fewer resources given to the intramural programs that serve the larger number of students.

One of the major initiatives that should be carried out, then, is an assessment of resource allocations provided for sports programs. Without strong, inclusive, well-funded intramural and interscholastic programs, it is impossible to involve large numbers of middle level students in the physical activities that they so deserve and need for healthy development.

In Summary

The overall plan for all middle level schools should clearly focus on the importance of comprehensive physical education classes, extensive inclusive and comprehensive intramurals, and a developmentally responsive interscholastic program.

This book focuses attention on middle school sports, an area that has received little attention over the last two decades. Herein we have (a) documented the status of sports programs in middle schools through a national survey; (b) reviewed the literature and research on middle school sports; and (c) examined selected issues facing middle school sports programs.

The ten recommendations in this final chapter provide a framework for schools to assess all aspects of their intramural and interscholastic sports programs. Ideally, these recommendations will stimulate discussion leading to specific actions improving their middle level sports programs.

The types of developmentally responsive programs described in this book can be achieved in every middle level school when the adults responsible for the education and welfare of young adolescents step forward with courage and determination, recognizing that the well-being of millions of young adolescents is at stake. ●

References

Abdal-Haqq, I. (2006). *Violence in sports*. Retrieved July 27, 2006, from http://www.childdevelopmentinfo.com/health_safety/violence_kids_sports.shtml

Alexander, W. M. (1968). *A survey of organizational patterns of reorganized middle schools*. Washington, DC: United States Department of Health, Education, and Welfare.

American Academy of Pediatrics. (2001). *Policy statement: Organized sports for children and preadolescents*. Retrieved June 1, 2006, from http://aappolicy.aappublications.org/cgi/content/full/pediatrics;107/6/1459

American Academy of Pediatrics. (2002). Supplement in *USA Today* (October 18-20). Sports injuries a growing problem in kids. Retrieved May 31, 2006, from http://www.aap.org/advocacy/releases/sportsinjury.htm

Anfara, V. A., Andrews, G., & Mertens, S. B. (Eds.). (2005). *The encyclopedia of middle grades education*. Greenwich, CT: Information Age Publishing.

Bigelow, B. (2000). Is your child too young for youth sports or is your adult too old? In Gerdy, J. R. (Ed.), *Sports in schools: The future of an institution* (pp. 7-17). New York: Teachers College Press.

Bigelow, B, Moroney, T., & Hall, L. (2001). *Just let the kids play: How to stop other adults from ruining your child's fun and success in youth sports*. Deerfield, FL: Health Communications.

Brown, J. (2000). When the fun goes out of the games. Special to the *Washington Post*. Retrieved June 2, 2006, from http://www.rowny.com/sportspsychotherapycenter/Jim_Brown.htm

Carey, B. (2006). *The most dangerous sports in America*. Retrieved June 1, 2006, from http://www.livescience.com/humanbiology/060614_sport_injuries.html

Cary, P. (2004, June 7). Fixing kids' sports. Rescuing children's games from crazed coaches and parents. *U.S. News & World Report, 136*(20), 44-53.

Cassas, K. J., & Cassettari-Wayhs, A. (2006). Childhood and adolescent sports-related overuse injuries. *American Family Physician*. Retrieved June 1, 2006, from http://www.aafp.org/afp/20060315/1014.html

Centers for Disease Control. (2002, August 23). *Nonfatal sports and recreation-related injuries treated in emergency departments: United States, July 2000 to June 2001*. Retrieved July 24, 2004, from http://www.cdc.gov/mmwr/preview/mmwrhtml/mm5133a2.htm

Coakley, J. (1987). Children and the sport socialization process. In D. Gould & M. Weiss (Eds.), *Advances in pediatric sports sciences*, (Vol. 2, pp. 43-60). Champaign, IL: Human Kinetics.

Coakley, J. (2004). *Sports in society: Issues and controversies*. New York: McGraw-Hill.

Darst, P. W., & Pangrazi, R. P. (2002). *Dynamic physical education for secondary school students*. San Francisco: Benjamin Cummings.

Dillion, N. (2006). Keeping students safe. *American School Board Journal, 193*(8), 15-19.

Educational Policies Commission. (1954). *Report of the Educational Policies Commission of N.E.A. and American Association of School Administrators*. Arlington, VA: American Association of School Administrators and Washington, DC: National Education Association.

Ellis, R. (2006). *Sports participation in children: When to begin?* Retrieved June 15, 2006, from http://www.sportssafety.org/articles/print/children-sports-participation

Engh, F. (2002). *Why Johnny hates sports: Why organized youth sports are failing our children and what we can do about it*. New York: Square One Publishers.

Erb, T. O. (Ed.) (2005). *This we believe in action*. Westerville, OH: National Middle School Association.

Ewing, M. E., & Seefeldt, V. (1989). *Participation and attrition patterns in American agency-sponsored and interscholastic sports: An executive summary.* North Palm Beach, FL: Sporting Goods Manufacturers Association.

Ferguson, A. (1999, July 12). Inside the crazy culture of kids sports. *Time, 154*(2), 52-60.

George, P. S., & Alexander, W. M. (2003). *The exemplary middle school* (3rd ed.). Belmont, CA: Wadsworth/Thomas Learning.

Georgiady, N. P., Riegle, J. D., & Romano, L. G. (1973). What are the characteristics of the middle school? In L. G. Romano, N. P Georgiady, & J. E. Heald (Eds.), *The middle school: Selected readings on an emerging school program.* Chicago: Nelson Hall.

Gerdy, J. R. (Ed.). (2000). *Sports in schools: The future of an institution.* New York: Teachers College Press.

Haggerty, M., & Odle, T. G. (2004). *Sports injuries.* Retrieved May 26, 2005, from http://www.healthatox.com

Hansen, J. H., & Hearn, A. C. (1971). *The middle school program.* Chicago: Rand McNally.

Health News (2006). From hoops to oops. Retrieved August 8, 2007, from http://www.iconocast.com/News_Files/HNews6_17_06/Health1.htm

Holm, H. L. (1996). Sport participation and withdrawal: A developmental motivational commentary. *Research in Middle Level Education Quarterly, 19*(3), 41-61.

Jackson, A. W., & Davis, G. (2000). *Turning points 2000: Educating adolescents in the 21st century.* New York: Teachers College Press.

Josephson Institute of Ethics. (2004). *New survey shows high school sports filled with cheating, improper gamesmanship and confusion about sportsmanship.* Retrieved August 7, 2007, from http://www.josephsoninstitute.org/

Kalodziej, A. (2006, June 23). Hoop dreams, or wake-up call? *The Columbus Dispatch,* pp. D1-2.

Legal Center: The Consumer Resource for Legal Information. (2005). *Sports law.* Retrieved June 3, 2005, from http://www.legalcenter.com/lc/sports-law.html

Mac, M. R. (1998, November). Managing the risks of school sports. *The School Administrator.* Retrieved June 3, 2005, from http://www.aasa.org/publications/sa/1998_11/Mac.htm

McEwin, C. K., & Dickinson, T. S. (1996). Placing young adolescents at risk in interscholastic sports programs. *The Clearing House, 69*(4), 217-221.

McEwin, C. K., & Dickinson, T. S. (1997). Interscholastic sports: A battle not fought. *Schools in the Middle: Theory into Practice, 6*(3), 17-23.

McEwin, C. K., & Dickinson, T. S. (1998). What role for middle school sports? *The School Administrator, 10*(55), 56-58.

McEwin, C. K., Dickinson, T. S., & Jacobson, M. G. (2004). *Programs and practices in K-8 schools: Do they meet the needs of young adolescents?* Westerville, OH: National Middle School Association.

McEwin, C. K., Dickinson, T. S., & Jenkins, D. M. (1996). *America's middle schools: Practices and progress—A twenty-five year perspective.* Westerville, OH: National Middle School Association.

McEwin, C. K., Dickinson, T. S., & Jenkins, D. M. (2003). *America's middle schools in the new century: Status and progress.* Westerville, OH: National Middle School Association.

Metzl, J. D., & Shookhoff, C. (2002). *The young athlete: A sports doctor's guide for parents.* New York: Little Brown.

Micheli, L. (2004, October 4). Overuse injuries: The new scourge of kid's sports. Children's Hospital Boston, *Pediatric Views.* Retrieved June 3, 2005, from http://www.childrenshospital.org/views/october04/overuse.html

Murphy, S. (1999). *The cheers and the tears: A healthy alternative to the dark side of youth sports today.* San Francisco: Jossey-Bass.

National Association for Sport and Physical Education. (2002). *Co-curricular physical activity and sport programs for middle school students: A position statement of National Association for Sport and Physical Education Council.* Retrieved July 30, 2005, from http://www.aahperd.org/naspe

National Education Association. (1952). *1952 Report of the Joint Committee of Representatives from the National Educational Association, The National Council of State Consultants in Elementary Education, the N.E.A. Department of Elementary Principals, the Society of State Directors of Health, Physical Education and Recreation.* Washington, DC: Author.

National Forum to Accelerate Middle Grades Reform (n.d.). *Vision Statement.* Retrieved June 14, 2005, from http://www.mgforum.org/about/vision.asp

National Middle School Association. (2003). *This we believe: Successful schools for young adolescents.* Westerville, OH: Author.

Noonan, D. (2003, September 22). When safety is the name of the game. *Newsweek, 142*(64), 64-66.

Ogilvie, B. C. (1988). The role of pediatric sports medicine specialists in youth sports. In J. A. Sullivan and W. A. Grana (Eds.), *The pediatric athlete* (pp. 81-89). Rosemont, IL: American Academy of Orthopedic Surgeons.

Patel, D. R. (2001, March). Youth sports: More than sprains and strains. *Contemporary Pediatrics.* Retrieved June 24, 2005, from http://www.aap.org/advocacy/releases/sportsinjury.htm

Romano, L, & Timmers, N. (1978). Middle school athletics—Intramurals or interscholastics? *Middle School Journal, 9(3),* 16-18.

Rotella, J., Hanson, T., & Coop, R. H. (1991). Burnout in youth sports, *The Elementary School Journal,* 91(5), 421-428.

Schenkenfelder. J. C. (2000). *It is our game: A guide for keeping youth sports in perspective.* Cleveland, OH: Greenleaf Book Group.

Seefeldt, V., Ewing, M, & Walk, S. (1993). *Overview of youth sports programs in the United States.* New York: Carnegie Council on Adolescent Development.

Stoker, S. E. (2000). *Preventing youth sport burnout.* Retrieved July 3, 2006, from http://selfhelpmagazine.com/articles/preventburnout.html

Swaim, J. H., & McEwin, C. K. (2005). Middle school sports. In V. A. Anfara, P. G. Andrews, & S. B. Mertens (Eds.), *Encyclopedia of middle level education* (pp. 347-353). Greenwich, CT: Information Age Publishing.

University of Maine. (2005). *Sports done right: A call to action on behalf of Maine's student-athletes.* Orono, ME: Author.

Vars, G. F. (1965). Change—and the junior high. *Educational Leadership, 23*(3), 187-189.

Votano, P. (2000). *The trouble with youth sports: What the problems are and how to solve them.* Westchester, NY: Xlibris.

Welsh, P. (2004). *One-sport athletes: A losing proposition for kids.* Retrieved August 7, 2007, from http://www.usatoday.com/news/opinion/columnist/2004-08-22-welsh_x.htm

Wolff, A. (2003, October 6). Are the games still fun? *Sports Illustrated, 99*(13), 59-67.